Handbook of Forms and Letters for Design Professionals

Handbook of Forms and Letters for Design Professionals

Society of Design Administration

WILEY

John Wiley & Sons, Inc.

Disclaimer

This publication is designed to provide accurate and authoritative information in regard to the subject matter covered. It is sold with the understanding that the publisher and the author are not engaged in rendering professional services. If professional advice or other expert assistance is required, the services of a competent professional person should be sought.

The Society of Design Administration has prepared this handbook as a resource for design firms. The society assumes no responsibility for the use of the forms, and recommends that all documents be carefully reviewed for legal accuracy according to state and federal law. The society, when referring to specific software or resources, is merely providing information and is not endorsing one product or person over another.

AIA, The American Institute of Architects and the AIA logo are registered trademarks and service marks of The American Institute of Architects.

This book is printed on acid-free paper. ∞

Copyright © 2004 by John Wiley & Sons, Inc. All rights reserved

Published by John Wiley & Sons, Inc., Hoboken, New Jersey

Published simultaneously in Canada

For general information on our other products and services or for technical support, please contact our Customer Care Department within the United States at (800) 762-2974, outside the United States at (317) 572-3993 or fax (317) 572-4002.

Wiley also publishes its books in a variety of electronic formats. Some content that appears in print may not be available in electronic books. For more information about Wiley products, visit our web site at www.wiley.com.

Library of Congress Cataloging-in-Publication Data
Handbook of forms and letters for design professionals / Society of Design
Administration.
    p. cm.
  Includes index.
  ISBN 0-471-26774-0 (cloth)
  1. Design services—Forms. 2. Design services—Marketing. I. Society of
Design Administration.
  NK1173.H36 2004
  729'.068'8—dc22

                            2004000672

Printed in the United States of America

10 9 8 7 6 5 4 3 2 1

Contents

CHAPTER ONE

The Writing Process

CHAPTER TWO

Administration

Accounting

Prebid Project Administration

CHAPTER FIVE

Bidding and Negotiation

CHAPTER SIX

Construction Administration and Post Construction

APPENDIX

Resources   231

Index   233

Preface

This handbook has been compiled to fulfill a recognized need within the design industry for a source of documents that are procedural in nature, many of which are not available as industry standards. The included forms, checklists, and spreadsheets were developed by small to large design firms from across the United States to address specific administrative or project-related needs. All contributions come from members of the Society of Design Administration (SDA) and are divided into chapters that focus on office administration, human resources, marketing, and accounting, as well as project administration requirements in the prebid, bid, construction, and postconstruction phases.

Although the majority of the documents provide a supplemental, administrative resource for procedural documentation and record keeping, a few are of a contractual nature. However, for contractual needs, it is highly recommended that design firms also review and consider the contract documents that are readily available through the American Institute of Architects, the Engineers Joint Contract Document Committee, and the International Federation of Consulting Engineers. Documents that are contractual in nature should come from a reliable professional source, or should be authored in conjunction with legal counsel. Specification-related information is also available through software prepared by both the American Institute of Architects and the Construction Specifications Institute.

The included documents support the myriad administrative tasks and design- and construction-related information that firms must record, often want to sort, and ultimately wish to track in a way that makes sense to the individual user. The purpose for many of the documents is self-explanatory, but each is accompanied by brief descriptions. Readers can access master and reference documents via the attached CD-ROM and are free to adjust formatting of the master documents according to their personal preference. As with the use of any master, it is recommended that users maintain the integrity of the master CD-ROM and use copied files to change formats to suit personal needs.

This handbook is organized in two parts—business requirements and project requirements. The six chapters progress from an overview of the writing process in Chapter One, including writing standards and office standards; to general administration in Chapter Two, including office administration, human resources, and marketing; to accounting in Chapter Three. Project administration needs are divided between the three final chapters and include pre-bid documents in Chapter Four, bidding and negotiation documents in Chapter Five, and construction administration and postconstruction in Chapter Six.

Most of the forms are straightforward and are shown blank. In a few cases where illustration is helpful, the form has been completed.

Acknowledgments

The Society of Design Administration wishes to recognize the many people who made contributions to the production of this handbook. The SDA is particularly grateful to the committee members who worked diligently to produce this publication, and recognizes the efforts of Chair, Brenda L. Richards, SDA, Hon. AIA, of DeStefano Architects, PLLC, Portsmouth, New Hampshire; as well as the contributions of the committee members who ably reviewed and edited the many submissions: Janet Bucholdt, SDA/C, of Shea, Minneapolis, Minnesota; and Deborah Rusnock, SDA/C, Principal, of Burke, Bales & Mills Associates, Lake Mary, Florida.

Well over 100 submissions were received from the following contributors: Jamie Achrazoglou, SDA/C, University of Iowa, Iowa City, Iowa; Angie Andujar, SDA, and Patsy Frost, Hon. AIA, SDA/C, of Schooley Caldwell Associates, Columbus, Ohio; Judy Beebe, SDA/C, of Parsons Brinckerhoff Quade & Douglas, Inc., Seattle, Washington; Gloria L. Boden, SDA/C, of Wakefield Beasley & Associates, Norcross, Georgia; Kay Boller, SDA/C, and Julie Severson, SDA, of Herbert Lewis Kruse Blunck Architecture, Des Moines, Iowa; Dee Broz, SDA/C, of Bahr Vermeer Haecker Architects, Lincoln, Nebraska; Ellen Blumenthal, SDA of Robert Silman Associates, PC, New York, New York; Ginger Castillo, SDA, of DeRevere & Associates, Newport Beach, California; David Church, SDA, of Moffat Kinoshita Architects Inc., Toronto, Canada; Betty Connell, SDA/C, of Island Architects, La Jolla, California; Beatrice Cook, SDA, Principal, JAED Corporation, Smyrna, Delaware; Stacia Cooper, SDA, Winter Street Architects, Salem, Massachusetts; Lisa DeStefano, AIA, Principal, and Jennifer Wiseman of DeStefano Architects, PLLC, Portsmouth, New Hampshire; Sally DiSciullo, SDA/C, Gallen Snow Associates, LLC, Denver, Colorado; Jackie Falla, SDA, of Tappé Associates, Boston, Massachusetts; Deloras M. Foster, SDA, of Cooper Carry, Inc., Alexandria, Virginia; Illona H. Iris, SDA, Design Services Group, Eden Pairie, Minnesota; Elaine Kalinowski, SDA/C, of Kinnison and Associates, Architects, San Antonio, Texas; Nickie Kearney, SDA, of CRB Consulting Engineers, Inc., Cary, North Carolina; Julie M. King, SDA, of Robbins Jorgensen Christopher, San Diego, California; Cher Lemaux, SDA, The IEF Group, Inc., Tucson, Arizona; Julie Meeks, SDA, Frank W. Neal & Associates, Inc., Fort Worth, Texas; Cheri Melillo, SDA/C, of Butler Rogers Baskett, New York, New York; Judy Merrill, SDA/C, of Nadel Architects, Inc., Costa Mesa, California; Sharon Nealy, SDA, Administrative Data Services, Clermont, Florida; Betsy Nickless, SDA/C,

Steven Langford Architects, Inc., Irvine, California; Joyce Pedersen, SDA/C, of PAA Architects & Planners, Inc., Tucson, Arizona; Kelly Perkins, SDA, AMEC Earth & Environmental, Inc., Portland, Oregon; Pat Potts, SDA/C, of M+O+A Architectural Partnership, Denver, Colorado; Stacy Rowland, SDA/C, of The Miller Hull Partnership, LLP, Seattle, Washington; Karen Roman, SDA/C, of Intergroup, Inc., Littleton, Colorado; Angel Sanford, SDA, of Pulley and Associates/Durant, West Des Moines, Iowa; Barbe Shaffer, SDA/C, CDT, of Baskerville & Son, P.C., Richmond, Virginia; Colleen Suite, SDA, of Brown Jurkowski Architectural Collaborative, PA, Raleigh, North Carolina; Liz Swize, SDA, of Emil G. Swize & Associates, Inc., San Antonio, Texas; Kathleen Thompson, SDA, Principal, of Pearce Brinkley Cease + Lee, PA, Raleigh, North Carolina; Susi Vestal, SDA/C, of Harthorne Hagen Architects, Seattle, Washington; Cindy Wait, SDA, of DMJMH+N, Inc. of Winter Park, Florida; and Gretchen Woodrick, SDA, of Small Kane Architects, PA, of Raleigh, North Carolina.

CHAPTER ONE

The Writing Process

Successful communication is three-tiered: visual, verbal, and written. All firms, but particularly design firms, give considerable thought to the visual image and design style that represents their public image in the form of letterhead and business cards, as well as their marketing pieces. But because designers are often gifted orators as well, they do not always give equal consideration to the writing style and documentation that supports the graphic and oral image.

The purpose of this handbook, therefore, is to provide a variety of writing samples and examples of forms and schedules used throughout the design and construction process. The information contained in the documents has been carefully selected and edited and the formatting is consistent and easy to convert to each firm's graphic style.

Clients, consultants, and coworkers will all appreciate documentation that is readable, correct, and consistent in style. An abundance of publications that support the mechanics of good writing are available. Two that writers will find invaluable are Strunk and White's *The Elements of Style* (Allyn & Bacon, 1999), and Manhard's *Goof-Proofer* (Fireside, Simon & Schuster, Inc., 1998). Each publication comprises 85 pages of precise, useful information. From cover to cover,

these texts serve as quick and easy-to-understand references.

Designers would not ignore structural details; neither should they ignore the details of good writing. They should develop the habit of looking up word usage and grammar, learn correct forms of address, and become familiar with the proper use of titles and honors. They should learn proper abbreviations and acronyms and use them correctly; and if correspondence crosses cultural borders, it is imperative that they research the etiquette that may be unique to communicating with foreign colleagues, clients, or vendors.

The principles of good writing should be incorporated into office standards as conscientiously as the parameters of good design are established as office standards. With both standards in place, continuity in design can be matched with continuity in written documentation. Almost everyone writes—from labels to e-mail, transmittals to general correspondence, meeting notes to change orders. Many people are involved in the process and have influence on the results. The practical way to simplify the basic parts of the writing process, and save time in the daily routine, is to provide templates for formatting and examples for style and content. Instituting writing standards and guidelines makes it possible to implement a systematic approach that improves efficiency and effectiveness. By establishing such standards within an organization, designers will be well on their way to maintaining the path to continual improvement.

In the design industry, the list of written documentation that can be generated is long. As expected in such a specialized industry, there are many unique documents. Some require the efforts of the full-fledged writing process, while others may require only filling in the blanks with appropriate words, phrases, or numbers. Each document should be referenced in the office standards and guidelines. Well-documented guidelines are continually updated so that all variety of correspondence and forms are easy to emulate.

EXAMPLE OF STANDARD GUIDELINES

Guidelines for Correspondence— [Designer & Associates, Inc.]

Introduction

[Designer & Associates, Inc.] has established these guidelines to promote the highest level of professionalism and consistency of format for all correspondence and written documentation. This includes letters, transmittals, meeting notes, spreadsheets, and other documentation that represents the company and its employees. It is our goal to make a notable impression on our clients, consultants, and other related business associates.

These guidelines are simple and direct. They are designed with the intent that employees can determine, at a glance—and in more detail, if desired—the standard format for the variety of correspondence used and distributed by the firm.

Letter Style

1. Block style: Left-justify only, with 1-inch margins around the body of the letter.
2. No indents, except as acceptable for displayed quotations, tables, and similar material.

Font Style

1. Arial 11 point throughout the body of the document.
2. Insert file name at 9 point.

Heading

1. Use embossed letterhead at top, left.
2. Date line:
   a. Position at second return, below letterhead logo.
   b. State month, date, and year, as shown (January 2, 2004).

Opening

1. Inside address:
   a. Position at third return below date line.
   b. If letter is addressed to two or more people at the same address, list each name on a separate line.
   c. If letter is addressed to two or more people at separate addresses, the individual inside addresses may be typed one under the other with one return between, or side by side in column format.

Sample Letter

Designer & Associates, Inc.
123 Maple Avenue
New Town, NY 10001
555-555-1234
555-555-9999 Fax
[
[
January 2, 2004
[
[
[
Mr. John Smith
Smith Engineers, Inc.
1234 Elm Street
Anytown, NY 10002
[
Via Facsimile: 555-555-1000
[
Subject: Letterhead Standards and Guidelines
            Project No. 100015
[
Dear John,
[
XXX XXXXXX XXXXXXXXX XXXXXXXXX XXXXXX XXX XXXXX XXXX XXXXX XXXXXX
XXXXXXX XXXXXX X XXXXX XX XXX. XXXXXX XXXX XXX XXXXX XXXXXXXX XXXXX
XXXXXXXX XXXX XXXX XX X XXXXXXXXXXXXXXX. XXXXX XXXXXX XX XX
XXXXXXX XXXXXXX XXXXX XXX XXXXXXXX XXXXX XXXXXXXX.   X XXXX XXX XXXX
XXXX XX XXXXXX XXX XX XXXX XXX XXXX XXXX XXXX XXXXX XXX XXXXX XXX
XXXXX XXXX XX XXX.
[
XXXXXXX X XXXXXXXXX XX XXXXXXX XXXXXXX XX XXXXXXXXXX X XXXXX
XXXXXXXXXX XXXX XXXXX XXXXXXX XXX X XXXXXX XX XXXXX XX XXXX XX
XXXX XXXXXXX XXXXXXXXX XXXX XXXX XXXXX. XX XXX XXX XXXXX XX X XXXX
XXXXXXX XXX XXXX XX X XXXXXXXXXXXXXXX. XXXXX XXXXXX XX XX X
XXXXX XXX XX XXXX XXX XXXX XXXX XXXX XXXXXX XXX XXXXX XXX XXXXXX XXXX
XX XXXXXXXXX XXXXXXX XXXX XXX XXXXXXXX XXXXX XXXXXXXX.   X XXXX XXX
XXXX XXXX X.
[
XXXXXXXX XXX XXXX XX X XXXXXXXXXXXXXXX. XXXXX XXXXXX XX XX X
XXXXXX XXX XXXX XXXX XXXXXX XXX XXXXX XXX XXXXXX XXXX XX XXXXXXXXX
XXXXXXX XXXX XXX XXXXXXXX XXXXX XXXXXXXX. X XXXX XXX XXXX XXXX X XX
XXXX XXX XXXX.

Second Page: Insert second page header and format as shown with name, date, and page number.

Mr. John Smith
January 2, 1004
Page 2
[
[
XX XXXX XXX XXXX. XXX XXXXXX XXXXXXXXX XXXXXXXXXX XXXXXX XXX XXXXX
XXXX XXXXX XXXXXX XXXXXXX XXXXXX X XXXXX XX XXX. XXXXX XXXX XXX
XXXXX XXXXXXXX XXXXX XXXXXXXX XXXX XXXX XX X XXXXXXXXXXXXXXXX.
XXXXX XXXXX XX XX XXXXXX XXXXXXX XXXX XXX XXXXXXXX XXXXX XXXXXXXX.
X XXXX XXX XXXX XXXX XX XXXXX XXX XX XXXX XXX XXXX XXXX XXXX XXXXXX
XXX XXXXX XXX XXXXXX XXXX XX XXX.
[
XXXXXXX X XXXXXXXXX XX XXXXXX XXXXXX XX XXXXXXXXX X XXXXX
XXXXXXXXXX XXXX XXXXX XXXXXXX XXX X XXXXXX XX XXXXX XX XXXX XX
XXXX XXXXXXX XXXXXXXXX XXXX XXXX XXXXX.
[
Sincerely,
[
DESIGNER & ASSOCIATES, INC.
[
[
[
[
John Q. Public
Principal
[
JQP/blr
[
Enclosure
[
c: X. XXXXXXXXXXXXX, Company
        X. XXXXXXXX, Company
        X. XXXXXXXXXXXX, Company
[
bc: X. XXXXXXXXX, Company
[
[
g:/arch/letter/smith

d. Do not abbreviate street, road or suite.
e. Per United States Postal Service standards, do not put periods after the letters indicating direction in address (e.g., NE, SW).
f. For foreign addresses, type country abbreviation in caps on separate line after city, state, and zip code.

2. Attention line:
a. Position at one return below inside address.
b. Do not abbreviate "Attention:"
c. To note "Personal," "Confidential," or a mailing notation such as "Via Facsimile," position notation at one return below inside address.

3. Reference or subject line:
a. Position at one return below attention line or mailing notation.
b. Use **bold** typeface.
c. Type out the word "Subject:" rather than the outdated Latin "Re."
d. Type "Project No. #" directly under the reference line, also in **bold** typeface.

4. Salutation:
a. Name (usually first name) followed by a comma and one return.
b. Use a colon after the salutation when a title and last name are used.
c. Use "Messrs." for two or more men, "Mesdames" for two or more women.

Body

1. Consists of the message for as many pages as is necessary.

Second Page

1. Header at upper left corner includes three lines of information:
a. Name of addressee
b. Date
c. Page number, typed as "Page #."

2. Insert one return and continue body of letter.

Closing

1. Signature block is positioned at one return after last line typed in body of letter and consists of the following parts:
a. Complimentary closing of "Sincerely."
b. Company signature, in this case, "Designer & Associates, Inc."
c. Writer's name and professional designation; for example, John Q. Public, AIA, or John Q. Public, PE.
d. Author's title, if appropriate; for example, Principal or President.

2. If appropriate, reference initials: initials of sender in caps, followed by forward slash and initials of keyboarder in lowercase; for example, JQP/blr.

3. Enclosure notation:
a. Position at one return below reference initials.
b. Spell out "Enclosure(s)."
c. If necessary for further clarity, list enclosed items by numbering and referencing each as follows:
1. Invoice No. 12344
2. Check No. 43213

4. Copy notation:
a. c:[TAB] name/company: Used to indicate that this person received only a photocopy of the letter.
b. c/enc:[TAB]: Used to indicate this person also received the attachments. If more than one attachment is enclosed, you may name documents within parentheses on the same line.
c. Use title (Mr., Ms., Dr.) before the name, followed by the name of the company (Dr. John Smith, General Hospital).

d. For blind copies, attach a list of persons blind-copied to the company file copy.

File Name

1. Place in footer, if possible, or at the bottom of each page.
2. If more than a one-page letter, do not show file name on the first page of the document.
   a. Font: Arial, 9 point, left-justified.
   b. Format: Lowercase; and show as drive/directory/file name as follows: g:/arch/letter/smith

Envelope

1. If letter is addressed to more than one person, send individual envelopes for each person, with full address and without reference to other recipient's names.
2. The following notation(s) may appear in the lower left of the envelope, in caps:
   CONFIDENTIAL
   PLEASE FORWARD
   HOLD FOR APPROVAL
   SPECIAL DELIVERY
   REGISTERED
   PERSONAL

General Notes for [Designer & Associates, Inc.] Documentation

1. Avoid abbreviations wherever possible.
2. Follow Information Systems Department protocol for naming a document. Do not create directories to "help" organize or separate files.
3. Use **bold**, *italics*, underlining, and CAPS only as necessary for reference or emphasis.
4. Do not staple multiple pages of letterhead. Use paperclips.
5. Use spell-check each time a change is made to a document.
6. Use the ampersand symbol (&) only as in a company logo.
7. Write out numbers one through nine. Show only two-digit numbers numerically.
8. When typing dollar amounts, use decimal (e.g., $500.00, not $500).
9. Do not allow date or individuals' names to wrap to the next line.
10. Use either a title before a name, or the degree or honor that may follow a name (Dr. John Smith, or John Smith, MD).
11. Follow Designer & Associates, Inc.'s standard abbreviation list for usual notations (e.g., square foot as SF, linear foot as LF) in each document.

A well-designed letter serves as the boilerplate for all further correspondence. If there is a good story to tell, tell it! Have fun with writing, and keep the following guidelines in mind:

- Stay with the topic.
- Do not mix verb tenses throughout the composition.
- Think about the promises being made and review contractual language with the proper legal resources.

- Consider style, format, and letterhead, and establish a suitable text format with typeface and font that is complementary. Formatting incorporates how the continuing pages will look, how sections will be defined, and how charts and photographs will be added to text. Once decided upon, address all of these points in the standards and guidelines.

- Pay attention to spelling and grammar—software cannot do it all.
- Build a library of reference materials for punctuation, usage, and style, and refer to the experts when unsure of a word or a phrase.

Note that the appendix in an up-to-date and comprehensive dictionary is a powerful resource, covering grammar and usage, as well as abbreviations, proper forms of address, foreign phrases, and much more; it is the primary resource you must have in your library. Other well-established and dependable reference publications, in addition to the aforementioned Strunk & White's *The Elements of Style* and Manhard's *Goof-Proofer,* are current editions of *Roget's Thesaurus,* and *The Gregg Reference Manual.*

To complement the variety of documents, forms, and schedules found in this handbook, review the many documents available in both written and electronic format from industry sources. The American Institute of Architects (AIA), national engineering societies, and national contractors' and builders' organizations all offer supportive information. In addition, financial and project management consultants sponsor seminars and publish a variety of guidelines for use in the design industry. There are programs that feature guidelines, outlines, and examples of business letters in the wide selection of current business software.

The samples, forms, and schedules in this handbook are meant to become useful tools for your office. Edit, format, and convert them to conform to your firm's graphic style, and use all of these resources wisely and effectively. Seek legal counsel to confirm that the verbiage and forms you select are appropriate for the services you provide and for the goals of your firm.

CHAPTER TWO

Administration

Saving the time it takes to "invent" appropriate documentation can enhance production and profitability. With that focus in mind, this chapter provides forms and letters appropriate for general office administration, human resources, and marketing, including some that overlap with accounting and project administration. The variety of forms and formats selected will serve users in a one-person design firm as well as staffs in medium and large firms. To embellish the individual contributions, copyrighted industry examples shown in this handbook are courtesy of the American Institute of Architects (AIA). As noted in the Introduction and the Appendix, several professional associations within the design industry also offer similar documents.

Over their years of practice, many design firms develop documentation that they feel is better suited to their specific needs. For example, several individually authored standard terms and conditions formats were submitted for publication; one is included. The AIA and other professional associations provide comprehensive contract documents (AIA B141-1977: Standard Form of Agreement between Owner and Architect) in which Standard Terms and Conditions of Contract are an integral part. Every design firm should consult with a legal advisor and carefully review contract choices.

By incorporating minor edits, several formats in this chapter are applicable to both general administration and project administration—notably, meeting notes, memorandum, telephone conversation report, transmittal forms, and the assignments form—and this is the case throughout the handbook. As forms are developed, incorporate new masters into office standards and guidelines and provide easy access to them through the office network.

All of the published documents are intended as supportive tools. To preserve that intention, it will be important to maintain the integrity of the CD-ROM by making edits and adjustments in separate files. Also, for the best and most effective use of each document, it is recommended that you review each one carefully and use proper legal discretion by seeking legal counsel *experienced in design and construction* to assure that wording is appropriate, legal, and suited to your firm's goals.

Interim Proposal

Using the proper legal discretion, firms may find this interim letter proposal adequate for the initial phase of a project, or as the agreement for projects with fees of $5,000 or less. An alternative to this letter agreement would be an industry standard contract such as the AIA B155-1993 Standard Form of Agreement between Owner and Architect for a Small Project.

Note: Review all contractual documents with legal counsel experienced in design and construction.

INTERIM PROPOSAL

Date

Subject: [Project Name and Project No.]

Proposal to: [   ]

This letter acknowledges the discussion at our meeting on [date] and will serve as an interim agreement for professional services for your proposed project located at [address].

To assist you in assessing the feasibility of the project, we agree to perform the specific services outlined below. If the project proceeds beyond the feasibility phase, it is understood that we will enter into a separate agreement for the continuation of the project into full design phases and documentation.

The general scope of work to be provided by [Designer] is as follows:
- Analysis of project requirements and site requirements with regard to access, utilities, zoning, and building code requirements.
- Preparation of three (3) design options in plan and sketch showing massing and location, vehicular and pedestrian circulation, and parking requirements.

The work performed by [Designer] shall be invoiced to you at our standard hourly rates as noted on the attached rate schedule. All reimbursable expenses (printing, mailing, etc.) will be invoiced at a rate of 1.15% of cost.

-OR-

We propose this work at a not to exceed fee of $_____, plus reimbursable expenses (printing, mailing, etc.) at a rate of 1.15% of cost.

If this proposal, along with the attached Contract Terms and Conditions, is acceptable, please sign below and return one copy for our records. Upon receipt of the signed Agreement and the retainer of $_____, we will schedule your work.

_____   _____
[Designer]   Date

_____   _____
[Client/Owner]   Date

Agreement for Design Services

Using the proper legal discretion, firms may use an industry standard contract such as the AIA B155-1993 Standard Form of Agreement between Owner and Architect for a Small Project.

Note: Review all contractual documents with legal counsel experienced in design and construction.

AIA® Document B155™ – 1993

Standard Form of Agreement Between Owner and Architect for a Small Project

This **AGREEMENT** is made:
(Date)

BETWEEN the Owner:

and the Architect:

for the following Project:

This document has important legal consequences. Consultation with an attorney is encouraged with respect to its completion or modification.

Because this document has important legal consequences, we encourage you to consult with an attorney before signing it. Some states mandate a cancellation period or require other specific disclosures, including warnings for home improvement contracts, when a document such as this will be used for Work on the Owner's personal residence. Your attorney should insert all language required by state or local law to be included in this Agreement. Such statements may be entered in the space provided below, or if required by law, above the signatures of the parties;.

The Owner and Architect agree as follows.

1

ARTICLE 1 ARCHITECT'S RESPONSIBILITIES

The Architect shall provide architectural services for the project, including normal structural, mechanical and electrical design services. Services shall be performed in a manner consistent with professional skill and care.

§ 1.1 During the Design Phase, the Architect shall perform the following tasks:
.1   describe the project requirements for the Owner's approval;
.2   develop a design solution based on the approved project requirements;
.3   upon the Owner's approval of the design solution, prepare Construction Documents indicating requirements for construction of the project;
.4   assist the Owner in filing documents required for the approval of governmental authorities; and
.5   assist the Owner in obtaining proposals and award contracts for construction.

§ 1.2 During the Construction Phase, the Architect shall act as the Owner's representative and provide administration of the Contract between the Owner and Contractor. The extent of the Architect's authority and responsibility during construction is described in this Agreement and in AIA Document A205, General Conditions of the Contract for Construction of a Small Project. Unless otherwise agreed, the Architect's services during construction include visiting the site, reviewing and certifying payments, reviewing the Contractor's submittals, rejecting nonconforming Work, and interpreting the Contract Documents.

ARTICLE 2 OWNER'S RESPONSIBILITIES
The Owner shall provide full information about the objectives, schedule, constraints and existing conditions of the project, and shall establish a budget with reasonable contingencies that meets the project requirements. The Owner shall furnish surveying, geotechnical engineering and environmental testing services upon request by the Architect. The Owner shall employ a contractor to perform the construction Work and to provide cost-estimating services. The Owner shall furnish for the benefit of the project all legal, accounting and insurance counseling services.

ARTICLE 3 USE OF ARCHITECT'S DOCUMENTS
Documents prepared by the Architect are instruments of service for use solely with respect to this project. The Architect shall retain all common law, statutory and other reserved rights, including the copyright. The Owner shall not reuse or permit the reuse of the Architect's documents except by mutual agreement in writing.

ARTICLE 4 TERMINATION, SUSPENSION OR ABANDONMENT
In the event of termination, suspension or abandonment of the project, the Architect shall be equitably compensated for services performed. Failure of the Owner to make payments to the Architect in accordance with this Agreement shall be considered substantial nonperformance and is sufficient cause for the Architect to either suspend or terminate services. Either the Architect or the Owner may terminate this Agreement after giving no less than seven days' written notice if the other party substantially fails to perform in accordance with the terms of this Agreement.

ARTICLE 5 MISCELLANEOUS PROVISIONS
§ 5.1 This Agreement shall be governed by the law of the location of the project.

§ 5.2 Terms in this Agreement shall have the same meaning as those in AIA Document A205, General Conditions of the Contract for Construction of a Small Project, current as of the date of this Agreement.

§ 5.3 The Owner and Architect, respectively, bind themselves, their partners, successors, assigns and legal representatives to this Agreement. Neither party to this Agreement shall assign the contract as a whole without written consent of the other.

§ 5.4 The Architect and Architect's consultants shall have no responsibility for the identification, discovery, presence, handling, removal or disposal of, or exposure of persons to, hazardous materials in any form at the project site.

ARTICLE 6 PAYMENTS AND COMPENSATION TO THE ARCHITECT
The Owner shall compensate the Architect as follows.

2

§ 6.1 The Architect's Compensation shall be:
(Indicate method of compensation.)

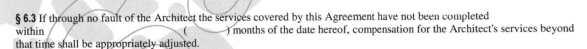

of which an initial payment retainer of   dollars ($) shall be
paid upon execution of this Agreement and shall be credited to the final payment.

§ 6.2 The Architect shall be reimbursed for expenses incurred in the interest of the project, plus an administrative fee
of   percent (%).
(List reimbursable items.)

§ 6.3 If through no fault of the Architect the services covered by this Agreement have not been completed
within   (   ) months of the date hereof, compensation for the Architect's services beyond
that time shall be appropriately adjusted.

§ 6.4 Payments are due and payable upon receipt of the Architect's invoice. Amounts unpaid
(   ) days after invoice date shall bear interest from the date payment is due at the rate of
percent (%) or in the absence thereof, at the legal rate prevailing at the principal place of business of the Architect.

*(Usury laws and requirements under the Federal Truth in Lending Act, similar state and local consumer credit laws and other
regulations at the Owner's and Architect's principal places of business, the location of the Project and elsewhere may affect
the validity of this provision.)*

§ 6.5 Architectural Services not covered by this Agreement include, among others, revisions due to changes in the scope,
quality or budget. The Architect shall be paid additional fees for these services based on the Architect's hourly rates when the
services are performed.

3

ARTICLE 7   OTHER PROVISIONS
(Insert descriptions of other services and modifications to the terms of this Agreement.)

This Agreement entered into as of the day and year first written above.
(If required by law, insert cancellation period, disclosures or other warning statements above the signatures.)

OWNER

ARCHITECT

_____
(Signature)

_____
(Signature)

_____
(Printed name and title)

_____
(Printed name and title)

CAUTION: You should sign an original AIA Contract Document, on which this text appears in RED. An original assures that changes will not be obscured.

4

Standard Terms and Conditions of Contract

Using the proper legal discretion, firms can use an industry standard document such as the AIA B141-1997 Standard Form of Agreement between Owner and Architect in which terms and conditions are an integral part.

Note: Review all contractual documents with legal counsel experienced in design and construction.

AIA® Document B141™ – 1997 Part 1

Standard Form of Agreement Between Owner and Architect
with Standard Form of Architect's Services

TABLE OF ARTICLES

1.1   **INITIAL INFORMATION**

1.2   **RESPONSIBILITIES OF THE PARTIES**

1.3   **TERMS AND CONDITIONS**

1.4   **SCOPE OF SERVICES AND OTHER SPECIAL TERMS AND CONDITIONS**

1.5   **COMPENSATION**

This document has important legal consequences. Consultation with an attorney is encouraged with respect to its completion or modification.

AGREEMENT made as of the   day of   in the year
(In words, indicate day, month and year)

BETWEEN the Architect's client identified as the Owner:
(Name, address and other information)

and the Architect:
(Name, address and other information)

For the following Project:
(Include detailed description of Project)

The Owner and Architect agree as follows:

1

ARTICLE 1.1 INITIAL INFORMATION

§ 1.1.1 This Agreement is based on the following information and assumptions.
(Note the disposition for the following items by inserting the requested information or a statement such as "not applicable," "unknown at time of execution" or "to be determined later by mutual agreement.")

§ 1.1.2 PROJECT PARAMETERS

§ 1.1.2.1 The objective or use is:
(Identify or describe, if appropriate, proposed use or goals.)

§ 1.1.2.2 The physical parameters are:
(Identify or describe, if appropriate, size, location, dimensions, or other pertinent information, such as geotechnical reports about the site.)

§ 1.1.2.3 The Owner's Program is:
(Identify documentation or state the manner in which the program will be developed.)

§ 1.1.2.4 The legal parameters are:
(Identify pertinent legal information, including, if appropriate, land surveys and legal descriptions and restrictions of the site.)

§ 1.1.2.5 The financial parameters are as follows:
    .1   Amount of the Owner's overall budget for the Project, including the Architect's compensation, is: unknown at time of execution of this Agreement
    .2   Amount of the Owner's budget for the Cost of the Work, excluding the Architect's compensation, is: unknown at time of execution of this Agreement

§ 1.1.2.6 The time parameters are:
(Identify, if appropriate, milestone dates, durations or fast track scheduling.)

§ 1.1.2.7 The proposed procurement or delivery method for the Project is:
(Identify method such as competitive bid, negotiated contract, or construction management.)

§ 1.1.2.8 Other parameters are:
(Identify special characteristics or needs of the Project such as energy, environmental or historic preservation requirements.)

2

§ 1.1.3 PROJECT TEAM

§ 1.1.3.1 The Owner's Designated Representative is:
(List name, address and other information.)

§ 1.1.3.2 The persons or entities, in addition to the Owner's Designated Representative, who are required to review the Architect's submittals to the Owner are:
(List name, address and other information.)

§ 1.1.3.3 The Owner's other consultants and contractors are:
(List discipline and, if known, identify them by name and address.)

§ 1.1.3.4 The Architect's Designated Representative is:
(List name, address and other information.)

§ 1.1.3.5 The consultants retained at the Architect's expense are:
(List discipline and, if known, identify them by name and address.)

§ 1.1.4 Other important initial information is:

§ 1.1.5 When the services under this Agreement include contract administration services, the General Conditions of the Contract for Construction shall be the edition of AIA Document A201 current as of the date of this Agreement, or as follows:

§ 1.1.6 The information contained in this Article 1.1 may be reasonably relied upon by the Owner and Architect in determining the Architect's compensation. Both parties, however, recognize that such information may change and, in that event, the Owner and the Architect shall negotiate appropriate adjustments in schedule, compensation and Change in Services in accordance with Section 1.3.3.

ARTICLE 1.2 RESPONSIBILITIES OF THE PARTIES

§ 1.2.1 The Owner and the Architect shall cooperate with one another to fulfill their respective obligations under this Agreement. Both parties shall endeavor to maintain good working relationships among all members of the Project team.

3

§ 1.2.2 OWNER

§ 1.2.2.1 Unless otherwise provided under this Agreement, the Owner shall provide full information in a timely manner regarding requirements for and limitations on the Project. The Owner shall furnish to the Architect, within 15 days after receipt of a written request, information necessary and relevant for the Architect to evaluate, give notice of or enforce lien rights.

§ 1.2.2.2 The Owner shall periodically update the budget for the Project, including that portion allocated for the Cost of the Work. The Owner shall not significantly increase or decrease the overall budget, the portion of the budget allocated for the Cost of the Work, or contingencies included in the overall budget or a portion of the budget, without the agreement of the Architect to a corresponding change in the Project scope and quality.

§ 1.2.2.3 The Owner's Designated Representative identified in Section 1.1.3 shall be authorized to act on the Owner's behalf with respect to the Project. The Owner or the Owner's Designated Representative shall render decisions in a timely manner pertaining to documents submitted by the Architect in order to avoid unreasonable delay in the orderly and sequential progress of the Architect's services.

§ 1.2.2.4 The Owner shall furnish the services of consultants other than those designated in Section 1.1.3 or authorize the Architect to furnish them as a Change in Services when such services are requested by the Architect and are reasonably required by the scope of the Project.

§ 1.2.2.5 Unless otherwise provided in this Agreement, the Owner shall furnish tests, inspections and reports required by law or the Contract Documents, such as structural, mechanical, and chemical tests, tests for air and water pollution, and tests for hazardous materials.

§ 1.2.2.6 The Owner shall furnish all legal, insurance and accounting services, including auditing services, that may be reasonably necessary at any time for the Project to meet the Owner's needs and interests.

§ 1.2.2.7 The Owner shall provide prompt written notice to the Architect if the Owner becomes aware of any fault or defect in the Project, including any errors, omissions or inconsistencies in the Architect's Instruments of Service.

§ 1.2.3 ARCHITECT

§ 1.2.3.1 The services performed by the Architect, Architect's employees and Architect's consultants shall be as enumerated in Article 1.4.

§ 1.2.3.2 The Architect's services shall be performed as expeditiously as is consistent with professional skill and care and the orderly progress of the Project. The Architect shall submit for the Owner's approval a schedule for the performance of the Architect's services which initially shall be consistent with the time periods established in Section 1.1.2.6 and which shall be adjusted, if necessary, as the Project proceeds. This schedule shall include allowances for periods of time required for the Owner's review, for the performance of the Owner's consultants, and for approval of submissions by authorities having jurisdiction over the Project. Time limits established by this schedule approved by the Owner shall not, except for reasonable cause, be exceeded by the Architect or Owner.

§ 1.2.3.3 The Architect's Designated Representative identified in Section 1.1.3 shall be authorized to act on the Architect's behalf with respect to the Project.

§ 1.2.3.4 The Architect shall maintain the confidentiality of information specifically designated as confidential by the Owner, unless withholding such information would violate the law, create the risk of significant harm to the public or prevent the Architect from establishing a claim or defense in an adjudicatory proceeding. The Architect shall require of the Architect's consultants similar agreements to maintain the confidentiality of information specifically designated as confidential by the Owner.

§ 1.2.3.5 Except with the Owner's knowledge and consent, the Architect shall not engage in any activity, or accept any employment, interest or contribution that would reasonably appear to compromise the Architect's professional judgment with respect to this Project.

§ 1.2.3.6 The Architect shall review laws, codes, and regulations applicable to the Architect's services. The Architect shall respond in the design of the Project to requirements imposed by governmental authorities having jurisdiction over the Project.

4

§ **1.2.3.7** The Architect shall be entitled to rely on the accuracy and completeness of services and information furnished by the Owner. The Architect shall provide prompt written notice to the Owner if the Architect becomes aware of any errors, omissions or inconsistencies in such services or information.

ARTICLE 1.3 TERMS AND CONDITIONS
§ 1.3.1 COST OF THE WORK
§ **1.3.1.1** The Cost of the Work shall be the total cost or, to the extent the Project is not completed, the estimated cost to the Owner of all elements of the Project designed or specified by the Architect.

§ **1.3.1.2** The Cost of the Work shall include the cost at current market rates of labor and materials furnished by the Owner and equipment designed, specified, selected or specially provided for by the Architect, including the costs of management or supervision of construction or installation provided by a separate construction manager or contractor, plus a reasonable allowance for their overhead and profit. In addition, a reasonable allowance for contingencies shall be included for market conditions at the time of bidding and for changes in the Work.

§ **1.3.1.3** The Cost of the Work does not include the compensation of the Architect and the Architect's consultants, the costs of the land, rights-of-way and financing or other costs that are the responsibility of the Owner.

§ 1.3.2 INSTRUMENTS OF SERVICE
§ **1.3.2.1** Drawings, specifications and other documents, including those in electronic form, prepared by the Architect and the Architect's consultants are Instruments of Service for use solely with respect to this Project. The Architect and the Architect's consultants shall be deemed the authors and owners of their respective Instruments of Service and shall retain all common law, statutory and other reserved rights, including copyrights.

§ **1.3.2.2** Upon execution of this Agreement, the Architect grants to the Owner a nonexclusive license to reproduce the Architect's Instruments of Service solely for purposes of constructing, using and maintaining the Project, provided that the Owner shall comply with all obligations, including prompt payment of all sums when due, under this Agreement. The Architect shall obtain similar nonexclusive licenses from the Architect's consultants consistent with this Agreement. Any termination of this Agreement prior to completion of the Project shall terminate this license. Upon such termination, the Owner shall refrain from making further reproductions of Instruments of Service and shall return to the Architect within seven days of termination all originals and reproductions in the Owner's possession or control. If and upon the date the Architect is adjudged in default of this Agreement, the foregoing license shall be deemed terminated and replaced by a second, nonexclusive license permitting the Owner to authorize other similarly credentialed design professionals to reproduce and, where permitted by law, to make changes, corrections or additions to the Instruments of Service solely for purposes of completing, using and maintaining the Project.

§ **1.3.2.3** Except for the licenses granted in Section 1.3.2.2, no other license or right shall be deemed granted or implied under this Agreement. The Owner shall not assign, delegate, sublicense, pledge or otherwise transfer any license granted herein to another party without the prior written agreement of the Architect. However, the Owner shall be permitted to authorize the Contractor, Subcontractors, Sub-subcontractors and material or equipment suppliers to reproduce applicable portions of the Instruments of Service appropriate to and for use in their execution of the Work by license granted in Section 1.3.2.2. Submission or distribution of Instruments of Service to meet official regulatory requirements or for similar purposes in connection with the Project is not to be construed as publication in derogation of the reserved rights of the Architect and the Architect's consultants. The Owner shall not use the Instruments of Service for future additions or alterations to this Project or for other projects, unless the Owner obtains the prior written agreement of the Architect and the Architect's consultants. Any unauthorized use of the Instruments of Service shall be at the Owner's sole risk and without liability to the Architect and the Architect's consultants.

§ **1.3.2.4** Prior to the Architect providing to the Owner any Instruments of Service in electronic form or the Owner providing to the Architect any electronic data for incorporation into the Instruments of Service, the Owner and the Architect shall by separate written agreement set forth the specific conditions governing the format of such Instruments of Service or electronic data, including any special limitations or licenses not otherwise provided in this Agreement.

§ 1.3.3 CHANGE IN SERVICES
§ **1.3.3.1** Change in Services of the Architect, including services required of the Architect's consultants, may be accomplished after execution of this Agreement, without invalidating the Agreement, if mutually agreed in writing, if required by circumstances beyond the Architect's control, or if the Architect's services are affected as described in Section 1.3.3.2. In the

5

absence of mutual agreement in writing, the Architect shall notify the Owner prior to providing such services. If the Owner deems that all or a part of such Change in Services is not required, the Owner shall give prompt written notice to the Architect, and the Architect shall have no obligation to provide those services. Except for a change due to the fault of the Architect, Change in Services of the Architect shall entitle the Architect to an adjustment in compensation pursuant to Section 1.5.2, and to any Reimbursable Expenses described in Section 1.3.9.2 and Section 1.5.5.

§ 1.3.3.2 If any of the following circumstances affect the Architect's services for the Project, the Architect shall be entitled to an appropriate adjustment in the Architect's schedule and compensation:

.1 change in the instructions or approvals given by the Owner that necessitate revisions in Instruments of Service;
.2 enactment or revision of codes, laws or regulations or official interpretations which necessitate changes to previously prepared Instruments of Service;
.3 decisions of the Owner not rendered in a timely manner;
.4 significant change in the Project including, but not limited to, size, quality, complexity, the Owner's schedule or budget, or procurement method;
.5 failure of performance on the part of the Owner or the Owner's consultants or contractors;
.6 preparation for and attendance at a public hearing, a dispute resolution proceeding or a legal proceeding except where the Architect is party thereto;
.7 change in the information contained in Article 1.1.

§ 1.3.4 MEDIATION
§ 1.3.4.1 Any claim, dispute or other matter in question arising out of or related to this Agreement shall be subject to mediation as a condition precedent to arbitration or the institution of legal or equitable proceedings by either party. If such matter relates to or is the subject of a lien arising out of the Architect's services, the Architect may proceed in accordance with applicable law to comply with the lien notice or filing deadlines prior to resolution of the matter by mediation or by arbitration.

§ 1.3.4.2 The Owner and Architect shall endeavor to resolve claims, disputes and other matters in question between them by mediation which, unless the parties mutually agree otherwise, shall be in accordance with the Construction Industry Mediation Rules of the American Arbitration Association currently in effect. Request for mediation shall be filed in writing with the other party to this Agreement and with the American Arbitration Association. The request may be made concurrently with the filing of a demand for arbitration but, in such event, mediation shall proceed in advance of arbitration or legal or equitable proceedings, which shall be stayed pending mediation for a period of 60 days from the date of filing, unless stayed for a longer period by agreement of the parties or court order.

§ 1.3.4.3 The parties shall share the mediator's fee and any filing fees equally. The mediation shall be held in the place where the Project is located, unless another location is mutually agreed upon. Agreements reached in mediation shall be enforceable as settlement agreements in any court having jurisdiction thereof.

§ 1.3.5 ARBITRATION
§ 1.3.5.1 Any claim, dispute or other matter in question arising out of or related to this Agreement shall be subject to arbitration. Prior to arbitration, the parties shall endeavor to resolve disputes by mediation in accordance with Section 1.3.4.

§ 1.3.5.2 Claims, disputes and other matters in question between the parties that are not resolved by mediation shall be decided by arbitration which, unless the parties mutually agree otherwise, shall be in accordance with the Construction Industry Arbitration Rules of the American Arbitration Association currently in effect. The demand for arbitration shall be filed in writing with the other party to this Agreement and with the American Arbitration Association.

§ 1.3.5.3 A demand for arbitration shall be made within a reasonable time after the claim, dispute or other matter in question has arisen. In no event shall the demand for arbitration be made after the date when institution of legal or equitable proceedings based on such claim, dispute or other matter in question would be barred by the applicable statute of limitations.

§ 1.3.5.4 No arbitration arising out of or relating to this Agreement shall include, by consolidation or joinder or in any other manner, an additional person or entity not a party to this Agreement, except by written consent containing a specific reference to this Agreement and signed by the Owner, Architect, and any other person or entity sought to be joined. Consent to arbitration involving an additional person or entity shall not constitute consent to arbitration of any claim, dispute or other matter in question not described in the written consent or with a person or entity not named or described therein. The foregoing

6

agreement to arbitrate and other agreements to arbitrate with an additional person or entity duly consented to by parties to this Agreement shall be specifically enforceable in accordance with applicable law in any court having jurisdiction thereof.

§ 1.3.5.5 The award rendered by the arbitrator or arbitrators shall be final, and judgment may be entered upon it in accordance with applicable law in any court having jurisdiction thereof.

§ 1.3.6 CLAIMS FOR CONSEQUENTIAL DAMAGES

The Architect and the Owner waive consequential damages for claims, disputes or other matters in question arising out of or relating to this Agreement. This mutual waiver is applicable, without limitation, to all consequential damages due to either party's termination in accordance with Section 1.3.8.

§ 1.3.7 MISCELLANEOUS PROVISIONS

§ 1.3.7.1 This Agreement shall be governed by the law of the principal place of business of the Architect, unless otherwise provided in Section 1.4.2.

§ 1.3.7.2 Terms in this Agreement shall have the same meaning as those in the edition of AIA Document A201, General Conditions of the Contract for Construction, current as of the date of this Agreement.

§ 1.3.7.3 Causes of action between the parties to this Agreement pertaining to acts or failures to act shall be deemed to have accrued and the applicable statutes of limitations shall commence to run not later than either the date of Substantial Completion for acts or failures to act occurring prior to Substantial Completion or the date of issuance of the final Certificate for Payment for acts or failures to act occurring after Substantial Completion. In no event shall such statutes of limitations commence to run any later than the date when the Architect's services are substantially completed.

§ 1.3.7.4 To the extent damages are covered by property insurance during construction, the Owner and the Architect waive all rights against each other and against the contractors, consultants, agents and employees of the other for damages, except such rights as they may have to the proceeds of such insurance as set forth in the edition of AIA Document A201, General Conditions of the Contract for Construction, current as of the date of this Agreement. The Owner or the Architect, as appropriate, shall require of the contractors, consultants, agents and employees of any of them similar waivers in favor of the other parties enumerated herein.

§ 1.3.7.5 Nothing contained in this Agreement shall create a contractual relationship with or a cause of action in favor of a third party against either the Owner or Architect.

§ 1.3.7.6 Unless otherwise provided in this Agreement, the Architect and Architect's consultants shall have no responsibility for the discovery, presence, handling, removal or disposal of or exposure of persons to hazardous materials or toxic substances in any form at the Project site.

§ 1.3.7.7 The Architect shall have the right to include photographic or artistic representations of the design of the Project among the Architect's promotional and professional materials. The Architect shall be given reasonable access to the completed Project to make such representations. However, the Architect's materials shall not include the Owner's confidential or proprietary information if the Owner has previously advised the Architect in writing of the specific information considered by the Owner to be confidential or proprietary. The Owner shall provide professional credit for the Architect in the Owner's promotional materials for the Project.

§ 1.3.7.8 If the Owner requests the Architect to execute certificates, the proposed language of such certificates shall be submitted to the Architect for review at least 14 days prior to the requested dates of execution. The Architect shall not be required to execute certificates that would require knowledge, services or responsibilities beyond the scope of this Agreement.

§ 1.3.7.9 The Owner and Architect, respectively, bind themselves, their partners, successors, assigns and legal representatives to the other party to this Agreement and to the partners, successors, assigns and legal representatives of such other party with respect to all covenants of this Agreement. Neither the Owner nor the Architect shall assign this Agreement without the written consent of the other, except that the Owner may assign this Agreement to an institutional lender providing financing for the Project. In such event, the lender shall assume the Owner's rights and obligations under this Agreement. The Architect shall execute all consents reasonably required to facilitate such assignment.

---

§ 1.3.8 TERMINATION OR SUSPENSION

§ 1.3.8.1 If the Owner fails to make payments to the Architect in accordance with this Agreement, such failure shall be considered substantial nonperformance and cause for termination or, at the Architect's option, cause for suspension of performance of services under this Agreement. If the Architect elects to suspend services, prior to suspension of services, the Architect shall give seven days' written notice to the Owner. In the event of a suspension of services, the Architect shall have no liability to the Owner for delay or damage caused the Owner because of such suspension of services. Before resuming services, the Architect shall be paid all sums due prior to suspension and any expenses incurred in the interruption and resumption of the Architect's services. The Architect's fees for the remaining services and the time schedules shall be equitably adjusted.

§ 1.3.8.2 If the Project is suspended by the Owner for more than 30 consecutive days, the Architect shall be compensated for services performed prior to notice of such suspension. When the Project is resumed, the Architect shall be compensated for expenses incurred in the interruption and resumption of the Architect's services. The Architect's fees for the remaining services and the time schedules shall be equitably adjusted.

§ 1.3.8.3 If the Project is suspended or the Architect's services are suspended for more than 90 consecutive days, the Architect may terminate this Agreement by giving not less than seven days' written notice.

§ 1.3.8.4 This Agreement may be terminated by either party upon not less than seven days' written notice should the other party fail substantially to perform in accordance with the terms of this Agreement through no fault of the party initiating the termination.

§ 1.3.8.5 This Agreement may be terminated by the Owner upon not less than seven days' written notice to the Architect for the Owner's convenience and without cause.

§ 1.3.8.6 In the event of termination not the fault of the Architect, the Architect shall be compensated for services performed prior to termination, together with Reimbursable Expenses then due and all Termination Expenses as defined in Section 1.3.8.7.

§ 1.3.8.7 Termination Expenses are in addition to compensation for the services of the Agreement and include expenses directly attributable to termination for which the Architect is not otherwise compensated, plus an amount for the Architect's anticipated profit on the value of the services not performed by the Architect.

§ 1.3.9 PAYMENTS TO THE ARCHITECT

§ 1.3.9.1 Payments on account of services rendered and for Reimbursable Expenses incurred shall be made monthly upon presentation of the Architect's statement of services. No deductions shall be made from the Architect's compensation on account of penalty, liquidated damages or other sums withheld from payments to contractors, or on account of the cost of changes in the Work other than those for which the Architect has been adjudged to be liable.

§ 1.3.9.2 Reimbursable Expenses are in addition to compensation for the Architect's services and include expenses incurred by the Architect and Architect's employees and consultants directly related to the Project, as identified in the following:

.1	transportation in connection with the Project, authorized out-of-town travel and subsistence, and electronic communications;
.2	fees paid for securing approval of authorities having jurisdiction over the Project;
.3	reproductions, plots, standard form documents, postage, handling and delivery of Instruments of Service;
.4	expense of overtime work requiring higher than regular rates if authorized in advance by the Owner;
.5	renderings, models and mock-ups requested by the Owner;
.6	expense of professional liability insurance dedicated exclusively to this Project or the expense of additional insurance coverage or limits requested by the Owner in excess of that normally carried by the Architect and the Architect's consultants;
.7	reimbursable expenses as designated in Section 1.5.5;
.8	other similar direct Project-related expenditures.

§ 1.3.9.3 Records of Reimbursable Expenses, of expenses pertaining to a Change in Services, and of services performed on the basis of hourly rates or a multiple of Direct Personnel Expense shall be available to the Owner or the Owner's authorized representative at mutually convenient times.

§ 1.3.9.4 Direct Personnel Expense is defined as the direct salaries of the Architect's personnel engaged on the Project and the portion of the cost of their mandatory and customary contributions and benefits related thereto, such as employment taxes and other statutory employee benefits, insurance, sick leave, holidays, vacations, employee retirement plans and similar contributions.

ARTICLE 1.4 SCOPE OF SERVICES AND OTHER SPECIAL TERMS AND CONDITIONS
§ 1.4.1 Enumeration of Parts of the Agreement. This Agreement represents the entire and integrated agreement between the Owner and the Architect and supersedes all prior negotiations, representations or agreements, either written or oral. This Agreement may be amended only by written instrument signed by both Owner and Architect. This Agreement comprises the documents listed below.

§ 1.4.1.1 Standard Form of Agreement Between Owner and Architect, AIA Document B141-1997.

§ 1.4.1.2 Standard Form of Architect's Services: Design and Contract Administration, AIA Document B141-1997, or as follows:
(List other documents, if any, delineating Architect's scope of services.)

§ 1.4.1.3 Other documents as follows:
(List other documents, if any, forming part of the Agreement.)

§ 1.4.2 Special Terms and Conditions. Special terms and conditions that modify this Agreement are as follows:

ARTICLE 1.5 COMPENSATION
§ 1.5.1 For the Architect's services as described under Article 1.4, compensation shall be computed as follows:

§ 1.5.2 If the services of the Architect are changed as described in Section 1.3.3.1, the Architect's compensation shall be adjusted. Such adjustment shall be calculated as described below or, if no method of adjustment is indicated in this Section 1.5.2, in an equitable manner.
(Insert basis of compensation, including rates and multiples of Direct Personnel Expense for Principals and employees, and identify Principals and classify employees, if required. Identify specific services to which particular methods of compensation apply.)

§ 1.5.3 For a Change in Services of the Architect's consultants, compensation shall be computed as a multiple of   (   ) times the amounts billed to the Architect for such services.

§ 1.5.4 For Reimbursable Expenses as described in Section 1.3.9.2, and any other items included in Section 1.5.5 as Reimbursable Expenses, the compensation shall be computed as a multiple of
(   ) times the expenses incurred by the Architect, and the Architect's employees and consultants.

§ 1.5.5 Other Reimbursable Expenses, if any, are as follows:

§ 1.5.6 The rates and multiples for services of the Architect and the Architect's consultants as set forth in this Agreement shall be adjusted in accordance with their normal salary review practices.

§ 1.5.7 An initial payment of   Dollars ($)
shall be made upon execution of this Agreement and is the minimum payment under this Agreement. It shall be credited to the Owner's account at final payment. Subsequent payments for services shall be made monthly, and where applicable, shall be in proportion to services performed on the basis set forth in this Agreement.

§ 1.5.8 Payments are due and payable   (   ) days from the date of the Architect's invoice. Amounts unpaid   (   ) days after the invoice date shall bear interest at the rate entered below, or in the absence thereof at the legal rate prevailing from time to time at the principal place of business of the Architect. *(Insert rate of interest agreed upon.)*

(Usury laws and requirements under the Federal Truth in Lending Act, similar state and local consumer credit laws and other regulations at the Owner's and Architect's principal places of business, the location of the Project and elsewhere may affect the validity of this provision. Specific legal advice should be obtained with respect to deletions or modifications, and also regarding requirements such as written disclosures or waivers.)

§ 1.5.9 If the services covered by this Agreement have not been completed within   (   ) months of the date hereof, through no fault of the Architect, extension of the Architect's services beyond that time shall be compensated as provided in Section 1.5.2.

This Agreement entered into as of the day and year first written above.

OWNER   **ARCHITECT**

_____   _____
(Signature)   *(Signature)*

_____   _____
(Printed name and title)   *(Printed name and title)*

CAUTION: You should sign an original AIA Contract Document, on which this text appears in RED. An original assures that changes will not be obscured.

10

Meeting/Conference Notes

This document is formatted for general administrative use, but could be used for project-related meetings and conferences, as well. Discussions and action items are recorded by the responsible person, who then can forward them to the appropriate parties, via hard copy or e-mail, for review or as the final document.

MEETING/CONFERENCE NOTES
No. ___

DATE: AUTHOR:

PROJECT No. _____   ATTENDEES:

PROJECT NAME:

MEETING LOCATION: COPIES TO:

NOTE: Any additions or corrections to these notes should be directed to the author within three (3) days
of receipt.
_____

PURPOSE OF MEETING:

ITEMS OF DISCUSSION:
1.

2.

3.

ACTION ITEMS:
1.

2.

3.

Memorandum

Standard format used to document corporate or project activities, share or release information, or make inquiries. Informal in nature, the memorandum can also be issued to serve as a reminder of decisions made and tasks to be completed.

MEMORANDUM

DATE:

TO:

FROM:

PROJECT:

PROJECT NO.:

SUBJECT:

COPIES TO:

SENT VIA: Fax   E-Mail   USPS   Overnight

COMMENTS:

This memorandum will be included in the project file. Notify the author of any omissions, additions, or clarifications within three (3) days of receipt.

Telephone Conversation Report

Basic format for documenting a conversation for inclusion in a permanent file, either administrative or project-related. The purpose of the report is to verify who made the call and why, and what was stated, questioned, or requested. The report can be used as a follow-up reminder to appropriate individuals.

TELEPHONE CONVERSATION REPORT

PROJECT:

DATE:

FROM:

COMPANY:

TO:

COPIES TO:

Any additions or corrections to this report should be directed to the author within 3 (three) days of receipt.

REMARKS:

Transmittal Letter

Standard format used to document the transmittal of corporate and project-related documents and information by facsimile, mail, or courier delivery.

TRANSMITTAL LETTER

To: Date:

                                       Project:
                                       Project No.:

Subject:
Attention:
Copies to:

We are sending you:

☐ Attached   ☐ Under separate cover   ☐ By hand

☐ Shop drawings   ☐ Prints   ☐ Plans   ☐ Specifications
☐ Change order   ☐ Submittals ☐ Certificate of payment
☐ Computer discs ☐ Copy of letter ☐ Application for payment

No. of Copies	Date	Drawing or ID No.	Description

This information is transmitted as noted below:

☐ For approval   ☐ As requested ☐ For review   ☐ For bids due   ☐ For your use
☐ Reviewed   ☐ Reviewed with notations   ☐ Approved   ☐ Rejected
☐ Revise and resubmit   ☐ Other
☐ By hand   ☐ By fax   ☐ By USPS   ☐ By overnight

Remarks:

Transmitted by: ☐ Fax   ☐ Messenger   ☐ Mail   ☐ Other

Letter of Transmittal

Use AIA Document G810 Transmittal Letter to document the transmittal or delivery of general information and project-related documents and information by mail or courier delivery.

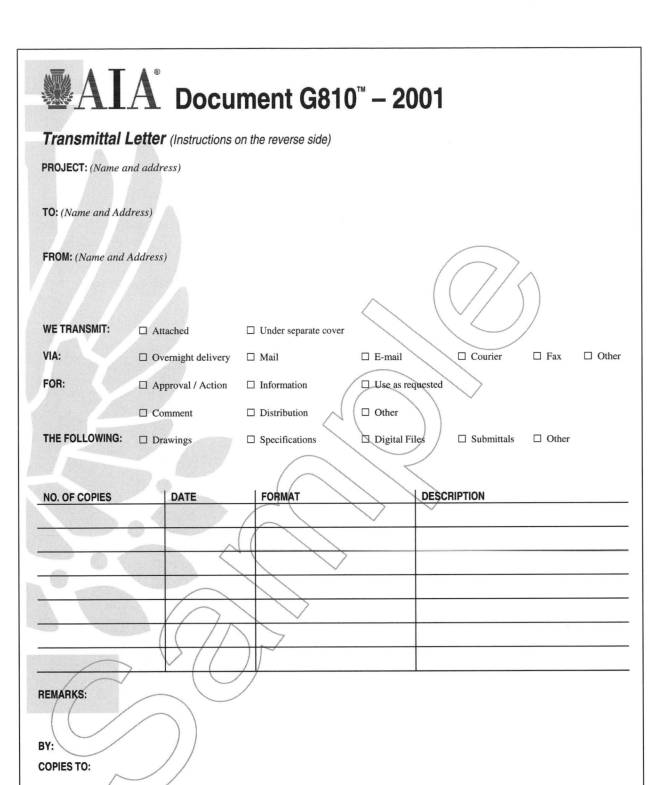

ΔIA® Document G810™ – 2001

Transmittal Letter (Instructions on the reverse side)

PROJECT: (Name and address)

TO: (Name and Address)

FROM: (Name and Address)

WE TRANSMIT:	☐ Attached	☐ Under separate cover			
VIA:	☐ Overnight delivery	☐ Mail	☐ E-mail	☐ Courier	☐ Fax ☐ Other
FOR:	☐ Approval / Action	☐ Information	☐ Use as requested		
	☐ Comment	☐ Distribution	☐ Other		
THE FOLLOWING:	☐ Drawings	☐ Specifications	☐ Digital Files	☐ Submittals	☐ Other

NO. OF COPIES	DATE	FORMAT	DESCRIPTION

REMARKS:

BY:

COPIES TO:

1

Fax Transmittal

Standard format used to document the transmittal of information or documents by facsimile. This document should be an office standard used by employees for each facsimile transmission.

FAX TRANSMITTAL

PROJECT:		PROJECT NO.:
DATE:		
NO. PAGES TRANSMITTED (including cover sheet):		
TO:		
FAX No.:		
FROM:		
COPY TO:		
ORIGINALS TO FOLLOW: ☐ YES ☐ NO		

REMARKS:

Sign-in Sheet

Use of this form will ease the task of tracking personnel and visitors. The sign-in sheet can be adapted for daily use by central reception to track personnel and visitors, as well as for in-house or job site meeting attendance.

SIGN-IN SHEET

Project: Date:

Project No.:   Location:

Purpose of Meeting:

Name	Company/Title	Phone	Fax	E-mail

Routing Template

Use this page of routing forms by clipping and attaching to correspondence, publications, and other items for in-house distribution. "Return to" and "date" fields should be completed.

Review, route and return to:	
LD	Library
JM	
JR	
JW	
BR	
TE	
DW	
DM	Date:

Review, route and return to:	
LD	Library
JM	
JR	
JW	
BR	
TE	
DW	
DM	Date:

Review, route and return to:	
LD	Library
JM	
JR	
JW	
BR	
TE	
DW	
DM	Date:

Review, route and return to:	
LD	Library
JM	
JR	
JW	
BR	
TE	
DW	
DM	Date:

Review, route and return to:	
LD	Library
JM	
JR	
JW	
BR	
TE	
DW	
DM	Date:

Review, route and return to:	
LD	Library
JM	
JR	
JW	
BR	
TE	
DW	
DM	Date:

Review, route and return to:	
LD	Library
JM	
JR	
JW	
BR	
TE	
DW	
DM	Date:

Review, route and return to:	
LD	Library
JM	
JR	
JW	
BR	
TE	
DW	
DM	Date:

Review, route and return to:	
LD	Library
JM	
JR	
JW	
BR	
TE	
DW	
DM	Date:

Review, route and return to:	
LD	Library
JM	
JR	
JW	
BR	
TE	
DW	
DM	Date:

Review, route and return to:	
LD	Library
JM	
JR	
JW	
BR	
TE	
DW	
DM	Date:

Review, route and return to:	
LD	Library
JM	
JR	
JW	
BR	
TE	
DW	
DM	Date:

Assignments Worksheet: Project/General

Supervisors, department heads, and project managers will find this form useful in documenting and tracking both project-related and administrative assignments and requests. It is a communication tool that can be used for daily tasks, as well as for long-term assignments and those requiring high-priority, special instructions, or background information. When used for high-priority or time-sensitive assignments, it is a good idea to copy the form on a distinctive colored paper to alert staff to its priority status.

ASSIGNMENTS WORKSHEET: PROJECT/GENERAL

Requested by: _____

Assigned to: _____

Project No.: _____   Date: _____

Project Name: _____

Task No.	Description	Action By	Date Due

Formatting Instructions		
Draft	Letter	
Final	Memo	
Double-space	Spreadsheet	
Single-space	Report	
Duplicate – Number of copies:		
HIGH PRIORITY – needed by – Date:	Time:	

Travel and Reservations Information Check List

This form can be edited to clearly specify the preferences and restrictions of a firm's corporate travel policies. It can be used as a record of standard information for each employee, or as the request and approval form for specific travel needs or for reservations. Office standards should denote who is qualified to approve travel requests and reservations.

TRAVEL AND RESERVATIONS INFORMATION

Request Date: _____   **Approved by:**_____

Employee: _____   **Approval Date:**_____

Project: _____   Reimbursable: Yes ___   No ___

Travel Information

Departure Date: _____   **Return Date:** _____

Reservation: Airline: _____   Train: _____

       Seating: Window: _____   Aisle: _____

Airport/Station: _____

Supersaver/Miles Account: _____

Ground Transportation: Rental car: _____   Limo: _____

Ticket/Reservation Received – Date: _____

Accommodation

Hotel: _____   **Check-In date:** _____ **Departure:** _____

Single; Queen Bed: _____

Business Discount Program: _____

Confirmation Received – Date: _____

Rental Car

Rental Company:_____   **Pick Up Date:** _____ **Drop Off:** _____

Discount Program: _____

Confirmation No.: _____   Confirmed Rate: _____

Directions to Destination Required? _____

Dining Reservations

Restaurant: _____

Number of Guests: _____

Date and Time: _____

Directions to destination required? _____

Sales Representative's Registry

Use this reference sheet to record contact information, track in-house visits by product representatives, and log samples and binders as received for project or library reference. When library space is at a premium, noting a Web address is adequate. File the registry pages in a three-ring binder and place it in the reference library for easy access.

SALES REPRESENTATIVE'S REGISTRY

REGISTRY NO. _____

Name _____   Telephone No. _____

Company _____   Office Hours _____

Address _____

Web Address_____

Who can answer technical questions or pricing information if you are unavailable?

Technical _____

Pricing _____

List products by generic titles and manufacturer, or be more descriptive, if necessary. List type of information as: samples, specification data sheets, catalog, or loose literature.

Product(s)/Manufacturer	Section No.	In-House Contact
_____	_____	_____
_____	_____	_____
_____	_____	_____
_____	_____	_____
_____	_____	_____
_____	_____	_____
_____	_____	_____

Please date this registry each visit. Review above information and update as necessary.

_____	_____	_____
_____	_____	_____
_____	_____	_____
_____	_____	_____
_____	_____	_____

Application for Employment

This application for employment can be edited to encompass the range of experience, skill levels, and education that have been set as standards for your design firm. Applicants will want to know that a firm is an Equal Opportunity Employer and whether the firm has an Affirmative Action program in place. If an Affirmative Action program has been developed and put in place, it can be noted as shown on page 1. Give each applicant a copy of the information they completed and signed. Following an interview, file the form in an appropriate human resources location. Many firms find it helpful to keep applications and accompanying resumes on file for a designated period of time, say six months, in anticipation of future job openings.

APPLICATION FOR EMPLOYMENT

This Firm is an Affirmative Action/Equal Opportunity Employer

Name _____ Date _____

Position Desired _____

Date Available _____

Address _____

Day Phone _____ Additional Phone _____

Social Security Number _____

Registration *(Arch.) (PE) (other), List States* _____

NCARB Certificate   ___ Yes ___ No

Professional/Civic Organizations and Activities _____

_____

EDUCATION

School Level	Name and Location	Last Year Attended	Did you Graduate?	Degree/Certificate
High School				
College/University				
Trade, Business or Correspondence School				

Applicant - complete as thoroughly as possible; skip any question you feel is not appropriate.

1 OF 3

Professional Experience: Note level of experience

Experience	Good	Average	Low	None	Experience	Good	Average	Low	None
Programming					Planning				
Design					Project Management				
Working Drawings					Cost Estimating				
Computer Aided Drafting					Delineation/Graphics				
Specifications					Clerical				
Construction Administration					Word Processing				
Interiors					Other:				

Employment History

Date From-To	Name of Employer, Address, Phone	Your Title, Duties/ Salary	Reason for Leaving	May be Contacted

References that may be contacted:

Name/Relationship	Address	Phone

Applicant - complete as thoroughly as possible; skip any question you feel is not appropriate.

I certify the accuracy of the information given on this application and grant permission for my references and former employers to be contacted, except as noted, in connection with the information on this application.

Signature:_____

Remarks:

Date Interviewed:_____ By:_____

Applicant - complete as thoroughly as possible; skip any question you feel is not appropriate.

Welcome Letter, New Employee

Even the most experienced of new employees will have questions while transitioning to his or her new workplace. This letter not only presents an agenda of first-day activities, but also sends a message of welcome, organization, and teamwork.

[Date]

WELCOME [new employee]:

Your first day of work is scheduled for _____, 20__. To help you become familiar with [company name], and to help you feel welcome, we have set up the following itinerary to make the transition into your new position as smooth as possible.

We are all pleased that you chose to join [company] or [department] or [branch office]. We are looking forward to seeing you on [day of the week] and have scheduled your day as follows.

9:15 a.m.   Meet with _____ and take a tour of the facility. You will receive a floor layout that shows office spaces, library, supply room, print room, and cafeteria.

10:00 a.m.   Administration/Human Resources processing with _____ includes review of benefits packages and enrollment forms, wage and payroll information, timesheets, parking options, and ID requirements.

11:00 a.m.   Computer processes with _____ to review standards and guidelines, e-mail, AutoCAD, directories, and web site.

12:00   Lunch with _____.

1:15 p.m.   Project review meeting with _____ to familiarize you with current work load.

2:30 p.m.   Time at your desk.

Your mentor is _____. Feel free to call your mentor or other members of the team with any questions you have.

Sincerely,

[Company Name]

[Name/HR Signature]

Orientation Check List

This new employee orientation check list can serve as a to-do list for a small firm's principal or administrator, or as a task list to assist the human resources department and supervisors in a large firm. The check list is established upon receipt of a signed offer letter. If a firm does not have an orientation guide or documented office standards, use this information as the basis of establishing appropriate documentation.

ORIENTATION CHECK LIST

Initial Activities   *(Administration/Human Resources)*

Prior to the arrival of [new employee], the following highlighted items should be accomplished and checked as completed.

- ❑ Sent offer letter [date]
- ❑ Received signed offer letter [date]
- ❑ Contact Supervisor of employee start date; inform Supervisor of role in orientation process
- ❑ Start personnel file folder
- ❑ Assign employee number
- ❑ Record new employee's social security number
- ❑ Forward SSN and start date to payroll service
- ❑ Establish workspace location
- ❑ Produce name plate for workspace
- ❑ Establish mailbox – inbox
- ❑ Verify computer for workspace
- ❑ Request/verify telephone, data jack, phone number with Information Technology
- ❑ Order cell phone set up, if necessary
- ❑ Supply workspace with calendar, updated reference lists, phone book, office supplies, including office keys
- ❑ Order business cards
- ❑ Coordinate e-mail and add new employee to list serves
- ❑ Schedule photo ID card
- ❑ Update phone list
- ❑ Update organizational chart
- ❑ Add new employee to agenda for monthly meeting/newsletter

Initial Activities   *(Supervisor)*

- ❑ Establish first day and first week agenda
- ❑ Edit and mail welcome letter and agendas
- ❑ Coordinate orientation
- ❑ Schedule new employee to attend meetings, as appropriate

First Day/First Week Agenda Checklist   *(Supervisor)*

The following are suggestions. The list should be customized for each new employee.

Agenda Item	Documents found in Orientation Guide
Supervisor ❑ General welcome discussion ❑ Introduction to company: mission, organization, history	❑ Mission statement ❑ Introductory letter ❑ Brochure ❑ Organization charts
Administration/Human Resources – *First Day* ❑ Employee data ❑ Tax information ❑ Orientation schedule ❑ Time sheet and procedures ❑ Benefits package ❑ Photo ID ❑ Parking options ❑ Signing in/out ❑ Payroll dates/delivery methods ❑ Equipment and supplies ❑ Credit card protocol	❑ Employee data worksheet ❑ Office manual ❑ Time sheet ❑ Phone extension list
General Tour ❑ Review of floor plan ❑ Introductions ❑ Survey of library ❑ Survey of supply area/mail room/print room	❑ Floor plan
Project Tour *(Supervisor or Project Manager)* ❑ Actual or virtual. ❑ Specific or general.	❑ Project list
Welcome Lunch *(Supervisor or assigned)*	
Information Systems *(ITS)* ❑ Directory structure and passwords ❑ Web site ❑ Software review ❑ AutoCAD *(if applicable)* ❑ Voice mail and password	❑ Directory chart ❑ System documentation

Corporate Methodology *(Human Resources and Supervisor)*	❑ Project management guidelines
❑ Project management processes	❑ Design standards manual, web location
❑ Design standards manual	
❑ Administrative and project forms, including time sheet	❑ Project flow chart
❑ Mentor program	❑ Requisition form

Employee Information

Use this format to record essential employee information, including positions held in the firm, salary history, and assignment of office equipment. Update the information on a regular basis. This form becomes a part of an employee's personnel file.

EMPLOYEE INFORMATION

NAME: _____   HIRE DATE: _____

ADDRESS: _____   BIRTHDATE: _____

_____   SS NO.: _____

HOME PHONE: _____   EMPLOYEE NO.: _____

CELL PHONE: _____   TERMINATION DATE: _____

EMERGENCY CONTACT: JOB TITLE:_____

NAME: _____

PHONE(S): _____

STATUS CHANGES:

	DATE POSITION/TITLE		DATE POSITION/TITLE
1.	_____	3.	_____
2.	_____	4.	_____

PAY CHANGES:

	DATE	SALARY		DATE	SALARY
1.	_____		4.	_____
2.	_____		5.	_____
3.	_____		6.	_____

OFFICE EQUIPMENT:

Office Keys: YES / NO   Parking Card No.: _____

Lap top: _____   Cell Phone: _____

Credit Card(s): _____

Other: _____

_____

NOTES:

_____

_____

_____

Employee Goal-Setting and Implementation Strategies

Distribute this simple goal-setting matrix to employees prior to their performance evaluation. Some firms find it helpful to have both employee and supervisor fill out the matrix, then compare results during the evaluation session.

EMPLOYEE GOAL-SETTING AND IMPLEMENTATION STRATEGIES

NAME: **DATE:**

CURRENT JOB RESPONSIBILITIES:

ACCOMPLISHMENTS OVER PAST YEAR:

GOALS FOR UPCOMING YEAR:	IMPLEMENTATION STRATEGIES:

Employee to complete and discuss with evaluator at time of evaluation.

Evaluation Date: _____

Employee Evaluation

Supervisors can use this form to document and appraise areas of employee responsibility, effort, and progress, in anticipation of employee evaluation. Evaluation suggestions should be measurable, and adequate time should be taken during the evaluation process to document performance fairly, in an effort to improve individual and firmwide results.

EMPLOYEE EVALUATION

Employee:

Evaluation Period From _____ **to** _____

<u>**Employee Performance Ratings**</u>

    5   Exceptional - Substantially exceeds requirements of the position.
    4   Above Average – Frequently exceeds requirements of the position.
    3   Average – Consistently meets requirements of the position.
    2   Fair – Does not consistently meet requirements of the position.
    1   Poor – Consistently fails to meet requirements of the position.

1.   <u>**Specific Performance Evaluation**</u>: Using the rating sheet, check the appropriate rating (1-5) for each appropriate item. Note comments to support the evaluation.

    a) **Quality of the work:** Ability to produce acceptable results with accuracy, thoroughness, and technical expertise.

        1 2 3 4 5   Comments: _____

    b) **Quantity of the work:** Volume of acceptable work produced. Efficiency and ability to organize and schedule work.

        1 2 3 4 5   Comments: _____

    c) **Knowledge of the work:** Basic understanding of job requirements and use of available technical resources. Shows interest and progress in professional development.

        1 2 3 4 5   Comments: _____

    d) **Work effort and initiative:** Initiative in learning technical concepts and methods. Willingness to contribute extended work effort. Willingness to further the goals of the firm.

        1 2 3 4 5   Comments: _____

    e) **Judgement:** Ability to identify, evaluate, and choose workable solutions to problems. Makes decisions that work.

        1 2 3 4 5   Comments: _____

    f) **Adaptability:** Supervision and time required to learn and internalize new tasks. Ability to adjust to change conditions. Adaptability to company policies and techniques. Attitude while performing tasks.

        1 2 3 4 5   Comments: _____

Page 1

g) **Dependability:** Ability to complete assignments on time with acceptable quality. Ability to concentrate on task. Assessment of time management skills.

1 2 3 4 5   Comments: _____

h) **Outside relationships:** Ability to maintain productive working relationships and supportive communication with clients and consultants.

1 2 3 4 5   Comments: _____

i) **Inter-office relationships:** Ability to relate to co-workers. Ability to accept and use constructive criticism. Relationship with superiors and team members.

1 2 3 4 5   Comments: _____

j) **Appearance:** Personal grooming, dress and deportment meet standards set for personnel and activities appropriate for employee's position.

1 2 3 4 5   Comments: _____

k) **Punctuality:** Keeps defined office hours for position. On time for meetings. Schedules meetings efficiently and appropriately.

1 2 3 4 5   Comments: _____

l) **Response to directions:** Ability to listen, accept direction, and perform according to directions given.

1 2 3 4 5   Comments: _____

m) **Leadership:** Relationship with co-workers and project participants. Ability to give directions, organize tasks, and achieve desired results.

1 2 3 4 5   Comments: _____

2)   **Specific Task Evaluation:** List major areas of position accountability, or tasks accomplished during review period. Briefly state results achieved in qualitative and/or quantitative terms. Evaluate results in each task.

Example: <u>Task</u>: Working on pre-design documentation for repeat client facing lengthy approval process.

<u>Result</u>: Followed an outlined procedure. Communicated well with client and city officials. Possesses technical abilities commensurate with work requirement.

Rating: 1 2 3 4 5

Page 2

Task: _____
Result: _____
_____
Rating: 1 2 3 4 5

Task: _____
Result: _____
_____
Rating: 1 2 3 4 5

Task: _____
Result: _____
_____
Rating: 1 2 3 4 5

3. **Summary of Performance Evaluation**
    1 2 3 4 5   Comments: _____
    _____
    _____
    _____
    _____
    _____

4. **Additional comments for discussion between employee and evaluator:**
    List comments regarding present position, aspirations, goals, and strategies.

    Personal strengths: _____
    _____

    Personal weaknesses: _____
    _____

    Firm's strengths affecting work: _____
    _____

    Firm's weaknesses affecting work: _____
    _____

    Personal goals: Short-term: _____
    _____

    Personal goals: Long-term: _____
    _____

    Miscellaneous comments: _____
    _____

    Comments on this Performance Evaluation: _____
    _____
    _____

    Page 3

I have read this Performance Evaluation and have discussed its contents with my reviewer and my supervisor. My signature indicates that I am aware of its content, but does not imply either agreement or disagreement.

Employee _____

Date _____

Reviewed By _____

Date _____

Page 4

Employee Termination Check List

Edit this check list to include specific information for your firm, such as return of all applicable equipment, COBRA documentation, and forwarding information, then have each terminated employee complete it.

Employee: _____ Social Security No.:_____

Forwarding Address: _____

Telephone: _____

Start Date:_____ Termination Date: _____

Reason for termination: Discharge   _____   Layoff _____
                              Leave of Absence_____
                              Resignation   _____   Letter of Resignation _____

Employee Submitted/Returned:

Final Time Sheet   _____   Key(s)   _____   Pertinent Files_____
Final Expense Report   _____   Credit Card(s)   _____   Drawings   _____
Cell Phone/Pager   _____   Parking Pass   _____

Administration Produced/Documented:
Final Pay Check:
Regular Pay   _____   Overtime Pay   _____
Vacation Hours   _____   Severance Pay   _____
Hand delivered on   _____   Mailed on   _____

Continuation (COBRA) Documentation For:

Health Insurance   _____   Long-term Care Insurance_____
Dental Insurance   _____   Other coverage_____

401(K) _____   Cafeteria Plan_____

Employee Signature: _____   Date: _____

Employer Representative: _____   Date: _____

Absence Request Form

Use this form to document requests for and approval of absence from work for overhead categories. Conference fees and travel funds can also be included for approval. Office standards should note who is authorized to give approval for time off or for funding.

ABSENCE REQUEST FORM

Employee: _____   Date:_____

Submit this form to [_____] for verification of time and $$ available. After approval, a copy will be returned to you.

Indicate category and hours for absence:

Project No./Phase Code		Hours Requested	Available
	Continuing Education		
	Community Service		
	Vacation		
	Personal - Sick		
	Other (please explain)		

If conference attendance or training time is being requested, describe briefly below and attach registration form.

	Date:	Schedule:		
First day of absence		Time out		
Last day of absence		Time return		
Date of return		Hours requested		

	Amount:			
Conference Costs:				
Air Fare:				
Meals:				
Ground Transportation:				
Total:				

Approved by: _____   Date: _____

This portion for Administrator's use:

	Available	Remaining
Professional Development	_____	_____
Community Service	_____	_____
Vacation	_____	_____
Personal - Sick	_____	_____
Expenses:		

Vacation Request Form

Project managers and supervisors can use this form to approve vacation hours and general absence for staff. This form also reminds staff that arrangements can be made with the payroll administrator to receive pay prior to the approved absence.

VACATION REQUEST

Date
submitted: _____

Employee _____ Studio/Dept. _____

Project
Manager _____ Approved on _____

Studio
Head/
Supervisor _____ Approved on _____

I plan to take vacation/be
absent from _____

to _____

I will return to work on

Emergency contact number _____

For Administration use only.

Total Proposed Vacation Hours ____	Total Proposed Hours of Absence ____
Vacation Hours Accrued to Date ____	Vacation Hours Accrued to Date ____
Balance ____	Balance ____
(overages to be deducted from next pay period)	(overages to be deducted from next pay period)

Note:
- Arrangements for receiving pay prior to a vacation or approved absence can be made with the payroll administrator by submitting this request at least two weeks before scheduled absence.
- Approval for absences shall be granted at the scheduling convenience of the firm.

Comments _____

_____

_____

_____

_____

_____

Proposal Request Form

Marketing personnel can use this form as a check list and as the record document for responses to Requests for Information (RFI), Requests for Qualifications (RFQ), and delivery of proposal packages to public and private sector agencies and owners.

PROPOSAL REQUEST FORM

Date RFI/RFQ/Proposal Request Received: _____

Date Information Due: _____

Number of submission sets required: _____

Deliver via: Messenger ☐   Fedex ☐   Mail ☐   Email ☐

Originating from: Main Office ☐   Branch Office ☐

Delivered to:_____

Attention: _____

Address: _____

Agency/Owner: _____

Phone: _____

Project Name: _____   Project No. _____

CBD Notice Date:_____

Project Type: Historic Preservation/Restoration ☐

                                      Survey/Investigation ☐

                                              Renovation ☐

                                       Adaptive Reuse ☐

                                  New Construction ☐

                                              Addition ☐

                                        Master Plan ☐

Items forwarded (with appropriate notes and date):

SF254 ☐   **SF255 ☐**   **SF330 ☐**

Firm Bio   ☐_____

Résumés   ☐_____

Relevant Experience ☐_____

Tear Sheets   ☐_____

Fee Schedule   ☐_____

References   ☐_____

Other   ☐_____

Comments:_____

Go/No-Go Evaluation

Adjust the questions on this form to suit your specific requirements and concerns and to evaluate the positive and negative aspects of working with a new client, developing a new geographic market, or undertaking a new project type. Valuable input during the evaluation process will come from principals, designers, technical staff, accounting, and marketing personnel.

GO/NO-GO EVALUATION

Give 1 point for each *yes*, 0 for each *no*. If the total is 7 or over, it's potentially a *go*; if less, it's a *no-go*.

Questions	Yes	No
1. Did the firm hear of the opportunity from an inside source (yes), or by public announcement (no)?		
2. Do we have an existing relationship with the prospective client?		
3. Is the client difficult to work with?		
4. Will the project fall into one of the firm's primary markets?		
5. Is this project an "investment" to help penetrate a new market?		
6. Does the firm have strong material to show at the interview?		
7. Is the fee commensurate with the project's technical complexity?		
8. Does the client have project financing in place that includes design fees?		
9. Is staff available to meet the necessary time commitments of the project?		
10. Do we understand the design problems and feel that we can perform well?		
11. Is there potential for repeat work? Does the client have existing relationships in the area?		
12. Will travel expenses incurred on the project be worthy of the profits or other goals (getting additional work or breaking into a new market) that may be achieved?		
13. If selected, are state and local approvals achievable?		
14.		
TOTAL:		

Business Development Matrix

Use this matrix to monitor ongoing business development tasks, critical due dates, and results on a monthly, quarterly, and annual basis. By adding items, lines, or pages, this form can accommodate comprehensive information.

BUSINESS DEVELOPMENT MATRIX

Date: _____   *Add new information in Italics.*
                                     Show on-going information in standard font.

INTERVIEWS

Interview Date/Time	Project/Owner	Location

PROPOSALS

Due Date	Project/Owner	Location

BUSINESS DEVELOPMENT

Date	Meeting/Walk Through/ Follow Up	Project/Owner

PRESS RELEASES

Date	Subject	Standard PR List/Add'l Contacts

PUBLICITY

Date	Subject	Publication

SUBMITTED PROPOSALS – FISCAL YEAR _____

Office/Commercial	Housing/Residential	Hospitality	Medical

CHAPTER THREE

Accounting

Even with the incorporation of comprehensive accounting software, many firms find that specially edited forms and spreadsheets are useful for monitoring finances, personnel hours, project profitability and productivity. For small firms operating on a cash basis, there are several cash position and budget forms that provide working documents for periodic accounting reports.

The spreadsheets shown in this chapter require a basic understanding of the formulas and cell activities that take place in a typical spreadsheet. It is recommended that, at the very least,

users take an on-line course in spreadsheet management. Familiarity with formula construction and cell requirements will make editing and adjusting for personal use easier and more effective.

Use good judgment in copying files from the CD-ROM and preserve the integrity of the original file until you become familiar with spreadsheet requirements. Once past the learning curve, you will find many ways to adjust these basic documents to make them even more useful.

Cash Receipts

Use the cash receipts form to manually document and calculate monthly cash receipts. This is a useful record for principals and accounting staff in small to medium firms, who wish to monitor cash receipts on a daily or weekly basis.

CASH RECEIPTS				12/29/03 5:28 PM
MONTH OF:				
Date	Project No.	Invoice No. Amount		Daily Total
Totals			$0.00	$0.00

Cash Out Monthly

Principals and accounting staff can use this form to document cash out (checks written) on a daily, weekly, or monthly basis.

CASH OUT			12/30/03 9:02 AM
MONTH OF:			
Date	Check #	Amount	Vendor/Type
Totals		$0.00	
		-$75,000.00	spending budget amount
		-$75,000.00	over/under budget

Cash Position Worksheet

To use the cash position worksheet to its best advantage, follow the work flow as prompts, and update on a daily or weekly basis.

CASH POSITION WORKSHEET

Month of:

CHECKING ACCOUNT [No.] BEGINNING BALANCE:			5,000.00
+ DEPOSITS:			
Date		1,500.00	
Date		0.00	
Date		500.00	
Date		0.00	
	TOTAL DEPOSITS	2,000.00	
SAVINGS TRANSFERS IN		0.00	
LINE OF CREDIT TRANSFERS IN		0.00	
TOTAL CASH IN FOR THE WEEK			2,000.00
- DISBURSEMENTS:			
CHECKS WRITTEN		(500.00)	
CONSULTANTS PAID		0.00	
PAYROLL		0.00	
TRANSFER TO SAVINGS		0.00	
LOC PAYDOWNS		(5,000.00)	
		0.00	
TOTAL CASH OUT FOR THE WEEK			(5,500.00)
CHECKING ACCOUNT (No.) ENDING BALANCE			1,500.00
SAVINGS ACCOUNT (No.) BEGINNING BALANCE		100.00	
+ DEPOSITS		0.00	
- DISBURSEMENTS		0.00	
+ INTEREST		0.00	
SAVINGS ACCOUNT (No.)+A17 ENDING BALANCE			100.00
TOTAL - CASH ENDING BALANCE			1,600.00

AP BREAKDOWN-to be paid by:	month ending (date)	week ending (date)	
ACCOUNTS PAYABLE (trade)	$500.00	(100.00)	
ACCOUNTS PAYABLE (subs)	$500.00	(500.00)	
PAYROLL	$0.00	0.00	
TOTAL ACCOUNTS PAYABLE			(600.00)
EXCESS OR (SHORTFALL)			1,000.00
Line of Credit ($10,000-$0.00=$10,000.00 balance available)			0.00
ANTICIPATED ACCOUNTS RECEIVABLE			13,000.00

Checkbook Ledger

Small firms operating on a cash basis may prefer to use this simple spreadsheet as a checkbook ledger.

CHECKBOOK LEDGER MONTH OF:_____			Deposits	Deposit Total	Balance Forward: Payments	1,000.00 Balance
Date	Check No.	Transaction Description				
4-Mar	10002	Petty Cash			50.00	950.00
						950.00
						950.00
						950.00
						950.00
						950.00
						950.00
						950.00
						950.00
						950.00
						950.00
						950.00
						950.00
						950.00
						950.00
						950.00
						950.00
						950.00
						950.00
						950.00
						950.00
						950.00
						950.00
						950.00
						950.00
						950.00
						950.00
						950.00
						950.00
						950.00
						950.00
						950.00
						950.00
						950.00
						950.00
						950.00
						950.00
						950.00
						950.00
						950.00
						950.00
						950.00
						950.00
						950.00
						950.00
						950.00
						950.00

Check Request Form

This form is formatted to simplify requests for and approval of payment by check of overhead and project-related expenses.

CHECK REQUEST

Payable to: _____   Date: _____

Amount: _____   Project: _____   Project No.: _____

Description: _____

Documentation
Attached: _____   Date Needed: _____

Requested by: _____   Approved By: _____

CHECK REQUEST

Payable to: _____   Date: _____

Amount: _____   Project: _____   Project No.: _____

Description: _____

Documentation
Attached: _____   Date Needed: _____

Requested by: _____   Approved By: _____

Direct Deposit Agreement

Payroll administrators can use this agreement to document an employee's direct deposit of pay to checking and savings accounts. Some payroll services will provide a similar form to their clients.

DIRECT DEPOSIT AGREEMENT

Name (as it appears on your check): _____

1. Bank Name: _____

    Account Number: _____

    Routing Number: _____

    $ or % to this Account _____

2. Bank Name: _____

    Account Number: _____

    Routing Number: _____

    $ or % to this Account _____

Payroll is not guaranteed until 24 hours after deposit date. If an accounting error should occur, we have the right to make appropriate corrections, including deducting funds. Such action will not take place without notification.

In order to verify personal banking information, please attach a copy of a check and/or deposit slip for the accounts you have listed above.

It is the employee's responsibility to notify the payroll administrator of any changes in banking documentation.

_____   _____

Employee Signature   Date

_____   _____

Payroll Administrator   Date

Date Keyed

Billing Schedule—Staff Hours Projection

Project managers can use this spreadsheet to calculate project staff requirements per project, per month. Fees and phase percent complete are entered in the Phase section. Billable hours are then reported per employee in the Billable Hours section. View cells to determine if they contain formulas and require numerical input.

BILLING SCHEDULE - STAFF HOURS PROJECTION

Project No.:

Project Name:

Contract Amount: $ 600,000.00

Month of: March, 20___

Phase	Phase Amt. (enter total fee $)	Phase % (For existing projects, enter "%complete")	Mar-03 (enter date)	Apr-03	May-03	Jun-03	Jul-03	Aug-03	Sep-03	Oct-03	Nov-03	Dec-03	Jan-04	Feb-04
Predesign	30,000	100.0%												
Schematic Design	90,000	75.0%	5.0%											
Design Development	90,000		5.0%											
Construction Docs.	270,000													
Construction Admin.	120,000													
Other*	0													
Fee Projection		97,560.00	9,000.00	0.00	0.00	0.00	0.00	0.00	0.00	0.00	0.00	0.00	0.00	0.00
Billable Hours		enter rates												
Principal		$ 120.00	4.0											
Sr. Project Manager		$ 105.00	3.0											
Project Manager		$ 95.00	2.0											
Drafter		$ 75.00	1.0											
Administrative		$ 40.00	0.0											
Billable Amount			1,060.00	0.00	0.00	0.00	0.00	0.00	0.00	0.00	0.00	0.00	0.00	0.00

Phase			Mar-04	Apr-04	May-04	Jun-04	Jul-04	Aug-04	Sep-04	Oct-04	Nov-04	Dec-04	Jan-05	Feb-05	Totals
Predesign	0														100.0%
Schematic Design	0														80.0%
Design Development	0														5.0%
Construction Docs.	0														0.0%
Construction Admin.	0														
Other	0														0.0%
Fee Projection			0.00	0.00	0.00	0.00	0.00	0.00	0.00	0.00	0.00	0.00	0.00	0.00	106,500.00
Billable Hours															Total Hrs.
Principal															4.00
Sr. Project Manager															3.00
Project Manager															2.00
Drafter															1.00
Administrative															
Billable Amount			0.00	0.00	0.00	0.00	0.00	0.00	0.00	0.00	0.00	0.00	0.00	0.00	1,060.00

Project Budget Worksheet—Residential

Use this spreadsheet to calculate total cost and value of a residential project. View cells to determine which cells require numerical input and which cells contain formulas. Insert firm profit percentage, as appropriate.

PROJECT BUDGET WORKSHEET—RESIDENTIAL

Project No.:

Project Name: Date:

A. Site Work	$15,000	$15,000
B. General Construction		$500,000
House - Main Level	$325,000	
House - Upper Level	$0	
House - Lower Level	$125,000	
Car Garage SF	$30,000	
Outbuildings	$20,000	
C. Exterior Improvements		$57,000
Hardscape (terrace, patios)	$20,000	
Pool, Spa	$15,000	
Fencing, Garden Walls	$10,000	
Site Lighting	$8,000	
Subsurface Drainage	$0	
Driveway Entry Accent	$4,000	
Tennis Court	$0	
Other Amenities	$0	
Landscaping		$25,000
Plantings, Site Preparation	$15,000	
Irrigation	$10,000	
Other	$0	
Permits		$13,000
General Building	$5,000	
Variances	$8,000	
Association Fees	$0	
Other	$0	
SUBTOTAL (C):	$95,000	
Architectural Fees		
Full Architectural Services (A+B+C)		$610,000
Profit (Sum of A, B, C above x 15%)	$91,500	
Reimbursables	$8,500	
Interiors		$40,000
Design Consultant	$40,000	
Item	$0	
Item	$0	
Item	$0	
Consultants		$55,000
Civil Engineer	$25,000	
Structural Engineer	$30,000	
Mechanical Engineer	$0	
Landscape Architect	$0	
Lighting Designer	$0	
Interior Designer	$0	
Other	$0	
Furnishings	$100,000	$100,000
SUBTOTAL:		$805,000
Finance	$0	$0
Land	$500,000	$500,000
PROJECT TOTAL:		$1,305,000

Project Budget Worksheet–General

Use this comprehensive budget worksheet to calculate allocation of fees and related labor requirements per project phase. Firm information is loaded in the shaded cells, and key formula changes are required for profit and indirect expense calculations. View all cells to understand formulas and numeric requirements.

Project No.:

Project Name:

Budget for Construction		$ 20,000,000
Basic Rate for Architectural Services		8%
Estimated Architectural Fee (Budget x Basic Rate)		$ 1,600,000

ALLOCATION OF FEES

Profit	15.0	% of Fee	$ 240,000
Structural Engineering	11.0	% of Fee	$ 176,000
M/E/P Engineering	22.0	% of Fee	$ 352,000
Civil Engineering	4.0	% of Fee	$ 64,000
Landscape Architect	2.0	% of Fee	$ 32,000
Environmental Consultant		% of Fee	$ -
Other Consultants		% of Fee	$ -
Direct Expenses (Other than Salaries)	0.3	% of Fee	$ 4,800
Indirect Expenses /1.73	0.3	% of Fee	$ 422,659
Direct Salary Expense	0.2	% of Fee	$ 308,541

ALLOCATION OF DIRECT SALARY EXPENSE

Project Administration	2	% of Fee =	$ 6,171	@	$ 50.00 Hr.	=	123 Hrs.
Master Planning		% of Fee =	$ -	@	$ 35.00 Hr.	=	0 Hrs.
Programming	4	% of Fee =	$ 12,342	@	$ 50.00 Hr.	=	247 Hrs.
Schematics	10	% of Fee =	$ 30,854	@	$ 40.00 Hr.	=	771 Hrs.
Design Development	15	% of Fee =	$ 46,281	@	$ 35.00 Hr.	=	1,322 Hrs.
Construction Documents	50	% of Fee =	$ 154,271	@	$ 25.00 Hr.	=	6,171 Hrs.
Specifications	2	% of Fee =	$ 6,171	@	$ 50.00 Hr.	=	123 Hrs.
Cost Estimating	2	% of Fee =	$ 6,171	@	$ 45.00 Hr.	=	137 Hrs.
Construction Admin.	10	% of Fee =	$ 30,854	@	$ 35.00 Hr.	=	882 Hrs.
Interior Design	5	% of Fee =	$ 15,427	@	$ 25.00 Hr.	=	617 Hrs.
Totals	**100**		**$ 308,541**		**$ 29.68** Avg $ /Hr.		**10,394** Hrs.

Project Budget—Bottom-Up

Project managers can use this spreadsheet to establish budget scenarios for new or ongoing projects. To begin the process, insert the total fee, profit percentage, direct consultant expenses, and nonreimbursable expenses in the appropriate cells. This generates the labor and overhead amount to calculate in this bottom-up spreadsheet. Next, insert the overhead factor (1.730 in this example), and the total labor cost will calculate. Then, insert percent per phase to generate the calculation of dollar values per phase. Finally, insert the per-hour wage average for the specific project team to generate the calculation of hours per phase.

Project: _____

Project No.: _____

PHASE		COST		HOURS
Preliminary Design	5%	$	1,643	88.1
Schematic Design	10%	$	3,286	176.2
Design Development	10%	$	3,286	176.2
Construction Documents	45%	$	14,786	792.8
Bidding	5%	$	1,643	88.1
Construction Administration	25%	$	8,214	440.4
Additional Services				
TOTAL LABOR COST	100%	$	32,857	1761.8
OVERHEAD FACTOR		$	1.730	
Per Hour Wage Average				$ 18.65
LABOR + OVERHEAD		$	89,700	

CONSULTANTS (DIRECT EXPENSES)		
M/E	$	45,000
Structural		
Landscape		
Civil		
TOTAL CONSULTANTS	$	45,000

NONREIMBURSABLE EXPENSES		
Fees		
Travel		
Printing	$	300
CADD Time		
TOTAL NONREIMBURSABLE EXPENSES	$	300

TOTAL LABOR & EXPENSES	$	135,000

TOTAL FEE	$	150,000
PROFIT	$	15,000
PROFIT PERCENTAGE		10%

Project Report—Actual to Budget Spreadsheet

Once a budget is determined and a project is underway, use this spreadsheet to help project managers and project teams track actual hours and dollars spent against budget estimates. This is a useful tool to monitor phase profitability and consultant expenses. View cells to determine if a cell contains a calculation or requires numerical input.

PROJECT REPORT - ACTUAL TO BUDGET

Project: SAVINGS BANK · Project No.::

	Prior Yr.	Jan	Feb	Mar	Apr	May	Jun	Jul	Aug	Sep	Oct	Nov	Dec	Totals	Cost	Budget Hr.	Budget $
LABOR PHASE																	
Pre Design	19.00													19.00	319.00	25.70	453.61
Sch. Design	34.00							34.00	1.00					69.00	1,418.00	51.40	907.21
Design Dev.								12.50	3.50					16.00	308.00	51.40	907.21
Const. Docs.	0.50						8.50	29.00	175.75	180.00				393.75	6,413.00	180.00	3,177.00
Bid														-		25.70	453.61
Const. Admin.									18.00	5.00				23.00	304.00	180.00	3,177.00
Additional														-			
TOTAL HRS.	53.50	-	-	-	-	-	8.50	75.50	198.25	185.00	-	-	-	520.75		514.20	
COST	1,019.00						103.00	1,302.00	3,183.00	3,155.00				8,762.00	8,762.00		9,075.63
OH (1.730)	1,762.87						141.52	1,788.95	4,373.44	4,334.97				12,038.99	12,038.99		12,469.92
Per Hr. Wage														16.83		17.65	
TOTAL $	2,781.87	-	-	-	-	-	244.52	3,090.95	7,556.44	7,489.97	-	-	-	20,800.99	20,800.99	0.97	21,545.55
CONSULTANTS														**Actual**	**Budget**		
M/E									2,037.50	1,862.50				3,900.00	3,900.00		
Structural									22.50					22.50			
Landscape														-			
Civil														-			
Reimb. Rec.														-			
TOTAL	-	-	-	-	-	-	-	-	2,060.00	1,862.50	-	-	-	3,922.50	3,900.00		
EXPENSES														**Actual**	**Budget**		
Travel	32.50						30.00	30.00	30.00	30.00				152.50			
Printing								21.00		939.23				960.23			
CADD Time	58.50						121.50	381.00	1,266.00	928.50				2,755.50			
Other Exp.							2.07	1.33	3.55	73.68				80.63			
Reimb. Rec.	91.00						153.57			3,757.77				4,002.34			
TOTAL	-	-	-	-	-	-	-	433.33	1,299.55	(1,786.36)	-	-	-	(53.48)			
														Actual	**Budget**		
TOTALS	2,781.87	-	-	-	-	-	244.52	3,524.28	10,915.99	7,566.11	-	-	-	24,670.01	25,445.55		
FEE BILLED	3,597.50	-	-	-	-	-	937.50			15,427.50	8,312.00	-	-	28,274.50	28,275.00		
PROFIT	815.63	-	-	-	-	-	692.98	(3,524.28)	(10,915.99)	7,861.39	8,312.00	-	-	3,604.49	2,829.45		
PROFIT %	0.23													0.13	0.10		

Reimbursable Expenses Log

If you do not have equipment that automatically tracks expenses by project number, post this form, along with a project list, near the task areas where reimbursable expenses are produced. To determine totals for billing purposes, use this spreadsheet as the calculator.

| Date | Project No. | No. of Copies | | No. of Plots | | | Cost of Film/Photos | Reimbursable | | Initials |
		8-1/2 x 11	11 x 17	11 X 17	24 X 36	30 X 42		Yes	No	

Employee Expense Form

Employees will find this spreadsheet helpful in tracking and calculating reimbursable expenses, whether overhead or project related. Notes that specify office standards (such as receipts required for payment) can be added.

Employee: _____   Employee #: _____

Date	Project No.	Phase Task/Code	No. of Miles	Mileage Rate	Mileage Amount	Park/Toll Amount*	Other*	Remarks/Purpose
				$ 0.365	-			
				$ 0.365	-			
				$ 0.365	-			
				$ 0.365	-			
				$ 0.365	-			
				$ 0.365	-			
				$ 0.365	-			
				$ 0.365	-			
				$ 0.365	-			
				$ 0.365	-			
				$ 0.365	-			
				$ 0.365	-			
				$ 0.365	-			
		SUBTOTAL REIMBURSABLES:			-	-	-	
		GRAND TOTAL:				-	

* Receipts must be attached to this form for payment to be made.

Consultant Tracking Spreadsheet

Use this spreadsheet to track consultant fees by manipulating the document to incoporate several projects per consultant, or several consultants per project.

JOB No.:   **PROJECT:**

COMPANY/CONSULTANT:
DISCIPLINE:
FEE: $ 50,000.00

DATE	INVOICE No.	% COMPLETE	FEE	BILLED TO DATE	FEE REMAINING	REIMBURSABLES
12/02/02	1	4.00%	$ 50,000.00	$ 2,000.00	$ 48,000.00	
01/03/03	2	9.00%	$ 50,000.00	$ 4,500.00	$ 45,500.00	
02/05/03	3	14.00%	$ 50,000.00	$ 7,000.00	$ 43,000.00	
03/04/03	4	20.00%	$ 50,000.00	$ 10,000.00	$ 40,000.00	$ 235.00
TOTAL FEE TO DATE:				$ 23,500.00		
TOTAL REIMBURSABLES TO DATE:						$ 235.00
TOTAL INVOICED TO DATE:					$ 23,735.00	

Simple Timesheet

This timesheet is a popular, simplified format. For convenience, an example of standard codes that could be used by a design firm is included in this file.

Firm Name
Address
Address

Employee: _____

Week Ending (Sat.): 2/27/2004 _____

Employee #: _____

Project #	Project Name	Task	Code	2/21 Sun	2/22 Mon	2/23 Tue	2/24 Wed	2/25 Thu	2/26 Fri	2/27 Sat	Proj.Tot
					1.00						1.00
						1.00					1.00
							1.00				1.00
								1.00			1.00
									1.00		1.00
										1.00	1.00
									1.00		1.00
								1.00			1.00
							1.00				1.00
						1.00					1.00
					1.00						1.00
				1.00							1.00
					1.00						1.00
						1.00					1.00
							1.00				1.00
								1.00			1.00
			Totals	1.00	3.00	3.00	3.00	3.00	2.00	1.00	16.00

Simple Timesheet Codes

TASKS

0 General
1 Predesign
2 Site Analysis
3 Schematic Design
4 Design Development
5 Construction Documents
6 Bid / Negotiate
7 Construction Administration
8 Post Construction
9 Supplemental

OVERHEAD PROJECT NUMBERS

1 General Overhead
2 Vacation
3 Personal
4 Holiday
5 Business Development
6 Marketing
7 Management
8 Accounting
9 Professional Development
10 Office Improvements
11 Word Processing

CODES

0 General
1 Site Analysis / Selection
2 Programming
3 Existing Facility Documentation
4 Project Administration
5 Client Meeting / Phone consultation
6 Materials Research / Selection
7 Estimating
8 Site Plan
9 Floor Plans
10 Elevations
11 Sections
12 Details
13 Consultant meeting
14 Specifications / Addenda
15 Shop Drawing Review
16 Site Meeting / Contractor Consultation
17 Post Construction Evaluation
18 Condo Association Meetings
19 Historic Distric Commisssion / Building Inspector
20 Zoning Board of Adjustments / Permits
21 Planning Board
22 Board of Directors
23 Special Presentation
24 Renderings, Models, Photography

Weekly Timesheet with Codes

Use this spreadsheet to record employee time on a weekly basis. Labor and task codes are listed for easy reference and can be adjusted to suit individual firm needs.

WEEKLY TIMESHEET

EMPLOYEE NAME

EMPLOYEE SIGNATURE

APPROVED BY

WEEK ENDING 28-Jun-03

PROJECT # or ADMIN CODE	LABOR CODE	REGULAR HOURS	OVERTIME HOURS	TASK CODE (WITH NOTES, IF REQUIRED)	S 6/22	S 6/23	M 6/24	T 6/25	W 6/26	Th 6/27	F 6/28
		0									
		0									
		0									
		0									
		0									
		0									
		0									
		0									
		0									
		0									
		0									
		0									
		0									
		0	**0**		0.0	0.0	0.0	0.0	0.0	0.0	0.0

KEYED

ADMIN CODES
ADMIN - GENERAL OVERHEAD
VAC - VACATION
PERS - SICK LEAVE
HOL - HOLIDAY
MKTG - BUSINESS DEVMT
PROF - PROFESS'L DEVMT
OTHER

LABOR CODES
01 - PREDESIGN/FIELD WK.
02 - PROGRAMING/PLANNING
03 - SCHEMATIC DESIGN
04 - DESIGN DEVELOPMENT
05 - CONSTRUCTION DOCS
06 - BIDDING/NEGOTIATIONS
07 - CONSTRUCTION ADMIN.
08 - QUALITY CONTROL
10 - SUPPLEMENTAL

TASK CODES
00 - GENERAL
01 - SITE ANALYSIS
08 - SITE PLAN
09 - FLOOR PLAN
10 - ELEVATIONS
11 - SECTIONS
12 - DETAILS
13 - CONSULTANT MEETING
28 - CODE REVIEW

CHAPTER FOUR

Prebid Project Administration

Managing the paperwork for a project from predesign through postconstruction is a challenge, and good communication and efficient record-keeping tools are vital to the successful management and completion of a project. The forms and spreadsheets specific to the predesign and design development phases run the gamut, from simple to complex, and may, with some imagination and manipulation, work well for project needs in subsequent design phases. For purposes of demonstration, the forms in this chapter are concise, but most can be expanded by item, line, and page to suit the requirements of even the most complex project.

Project record-keeping and in-house approvals are generally the responsibility of project managers or accounting staff. In all instances where approval is required for distribution or payment, it should be clearly noted on forms. As project teams are developed, and documents are formatted for specific projects, the personnel responsible for approvals also should be noted, as part of the initialization process.

As an example of the usefulness of the forms supplied in this chapter, consider that a key factor to success in the predesign phase is the presentation of a comprehensive programming report. This chapter includes seven programming documents that, when completed, will provide the information needed to develop a useful programming report. The process is as follows:

1. Complete Parts A and A.1.
2. Assign completion of Parts B through E to the appropriate design team and client personnel.
3. Follow the instructions for each part, reviewing client/user needs, and comments.
4. Organize the information in a manner that is useful to both the client and the design team.

By taking these steps, you can easily compose the programming report. And, by adding information discovered through the completion of the Code Research and Requirements matrix for code requirements and approval processes, you can present a substantial predesign document to the client.

Project Directory

AIA Document G807 Project Team Directory contains general project information, as well as consultants' contact data. This information can be shared among project managers, administrators, and marketing personnel. Additional information, such as Web addresses and cell phone numbers, could be added.

Document G807™ – 2001

Project Team Directory *(Instructions on the reverse side)*

PROJECT: *(Name and address)*   **PROJECT NUMBER:**

(Indicate firm name, address, and telephone and fax numbers, as well as an e-mail address, for each Project Team participant listed below)

OWNER:

Designated Representative:

Reviewers of Architect's Submittals:

Attorneys:

Insurance Advisors:

Accountants:

Owner's Consultants:

Owner's Separate Contractors:

ARCHITECT:

Architect's Designated Representative:

Project Architect/Manager:

Architect's Consultants:

CONTRACTORS *(Indicate general and other prime contractors, if any)*:

1

Contract Administration

AIA Document G809, Project Abstract, includes project information regarding phases, finances, and consultants. It is to be completed by the project manager, then distributed, as appropriate, to administrative, accounting, and marketing staff. It may be useful to have a centrally located, three-ring binder that contains the up-to-date project information. Generally, it is the responsibility of the project manager to update and redistribute as the project history changes.

∆I∆® Document G809™ – 2001

Project Abstract *(Instructions on the reverse side)*

PROJECT: *(Name and address)*

PROJECT NUMBER:
DATE:
ABSTRACT STATUS: ☒ IN PROGRESS ☐ CLOSED OUT

PROJECT TYPE:
☐ Institutional ☐ Industrial ☐ Residential ☐ Other

PROJECT SIZE *(Square feet)*:

BUILDING COST:

PROJECT SCOPE:

COST OF SITE WORK:

CURRENT PROJECT STATUS: ☐ Design ☐ Under Construction
☐ Procurement ☐ Completed

DATE OF SUBSTANTIAL COMPLETION:

DATE OF FINAL COMPLETION:

OWNER *(Name and address)*:

OWNER'S DESIGNATED REPRESENTATIVE *(Name and address)*:

CONTRACTOR *(Name and address)*:

CONTRACTOR'S DESIGNATED REPRESENTATIVE *(Name and address)*:

PROCUREMENT METHOD:

ARCHITECT *(Name and address)*:

CONSULTANTS
Civil *(Name)*:
Landscape *(Name)*:
Structural *(Name)*:
MEP *(Name)*:
Interiors *(Name)*:
Others *(Name)*:

PRINCIPAL IN CHARGE *(Name)*:
PROJECT ARCHITECT/MANAGER *(Name)*:
PROJECT STAFF *(Name)*:

Will we use this project for marketing? ☐ Yes ☐ No
Do we want a detailed account of the change orders? ☐ Yes ☐ No
Do we want to include in SF254 Profile statistics? ☐ Yes ☐ No

SF254 Profile Codes *(List all applicable)*:

1

Project Information Start-up Check List

This check list serves as a "tickler" file for project start-up information pertinent to project managers, to the team members responsible for accounting and marketing details, and to the project administrator.

PROJECT INFORMATION START-UP CHECK LIST

Project:_____ Project No.:_____

Principal:_____ Project Manager:_____

☐ **Project Information Entered for Billing**

Client Name and Address_____

_____

Billing Address (if different from above)_____

_____

Project Folder in Computer System

☐ Date activated_____

Project Management Files Required

Incoming correspondence

☐ Outgoing correspondence

☐ Contract/Invoices

☐ Consultants, as noted:_____

Signed Contracts

☐ Client – dated_____

☐ Consultants – Name and date of receipt

_____

_____

_____

_____

☐ **1099 Information (if not a corporation)**

☐ **Certificate(s) of Insurance to Client** – Professional Liability_____

General Liability_____   Auto_____   Worker's Compensation_____

☐ **Certificate of Insurance from Consultants**

☐ Consultants – Name and date of receipt

_____

_____

_____

Certificate of Insurance Request

This letter template contains basic information to request a certificate of insurance from a consultant. It can also be used to make a general request of vendors and other service providers, as appropriate.

Date

Name
Company
Street
City, State, Zip

Subject: Request for Certificate of Insurance

To update our records, and to be in compliance with the terms of our contract/agreement for [project description], we request current Certificates of Insurance from you as noted below:

☐ General Liability
☐ Workers Compensation
☐ Automobile Coverage
☐ Professional Liability

In addition, we request that you name [Company] as Additional Insured.

Please have the Certificate(s) forwarded to:

[Designer]
Address
Address

Do not hesitate to call [   ], the contract administrator, with any questions.

Sincerely,

[Company Name]

[Signer's Name]

[Reference Initials]

Certificate of Insurance Log

Project administrators can use this log to record requests for and receipt of certificates of insurance. One log can serve all in-house projects, or, for larger projects, logs can be sorted by individual project numbers. Notation of expiration dates will prompt renewal requests.

Certificate of Insurance Log

Project No.:

Company/Consultant	Date Requested	Date Received	Professional Liability	Workers Compensation	General Liabiltiy	Auto	Renewal Date

Meeting Minutes Template

Use this template to document all discussions at project-related meetings, whether on- or off-site. Note actions as approved or required, as well as actions completed since the previous project meeting. Generally, project managers take the meeting minutes, but the task may be delegated to a project engineer or architect, with the project manager taking responsibility for final approval prior to distribution.

	Project No.:	**xxxx**
	Meeting Minutes No.:	**xxx**
	Meeting Date:	**xx/xx/xx**
	Issue Date:	**xx/xx/xx**

MEETING MINUTES NO. [   ]

The contents of these minutes are assumed to be correct unless [Designer] is notified, in writing, of any additions, corrections, or deletions within three (3) calendar days of receipt.

MEETING MINUTES TEMPLATE

Project: [Project Name]

Meeting: [Subject or Type of Meeting]

Location: [Meeting Location]

Attendees: [Name] [Firm]   [Name] [Firm]
                        [Name] [Firm]   [Name] [Firm]

Author: [Author of Minutes]

Distribution: All present   [Name] [Firm]

For corrections or clarifications, contact: [Name]

Item	Action*	Discussion
1.1	AR: Note short definition of action required.	Items are numbered as meeting minutes progress. For example, the second meeting would produce Meeting Minutes No. 2 and the Items would be listed as 2.1, 2.2, 2.3. The third set of minutes would be Meeting Minutes No. 3 and the Items would be listed as 3.1, 3.2, 3.3. To change this template, go to "Format," "Bullets and Numbering, " "Numbered Tab," and select the related setting. Then, change the preceding number in the Number Format window.
1.2		To insert rows in the table, go to "Table," "Insert Rows."
1.3		To hide the lines in this table, place the cursor somewhere inside the table, go to "Table," "Hide Gridlines."
1.4		First and second page headers may differ. The header information on the second page can be formatted to relate to each meeting minute template.

<u>END OF MINUTES</u>

* AC = Action Complete   AA = Action approved   AR = Action required

Travel Log

Project teams can use this spreadsheet to document travel and related expenses for site visits and miscellaneous project activities. Approval is required by the principal or project manager prior to submission for payment or posting of charge to project budget.

TRAVEL LOG

PROJECT NAME   *enter name here*
PROJECT NO.   *enter number here*

VISIT NO.	DATE	REQUESTED BY	REASON FOR TRIP	PERSON(S) TRAVELING	EXPENSES INCURRED	APPROVED BY (Initial)
1	06/19/04	Contractor	Review of site condition			
2						
3						
4						
5						
6						
7						
8						
9						
10						
11						
12						
13						
14						
15						
16						
17						
18						
19						
20						
21						
22						
23						
24						
25						
26						
27						
28						
29						
30						
31						
32						
33						
34						
35						
36						
37						
38						
39						
40						

Code Research and Requirements

Completion of this predesign phase form, AIA Document G808, Project Data, generally requires contributions from various members of the project team. One designated person, however, should hold responsibility for final completion and for time-sensitive results.

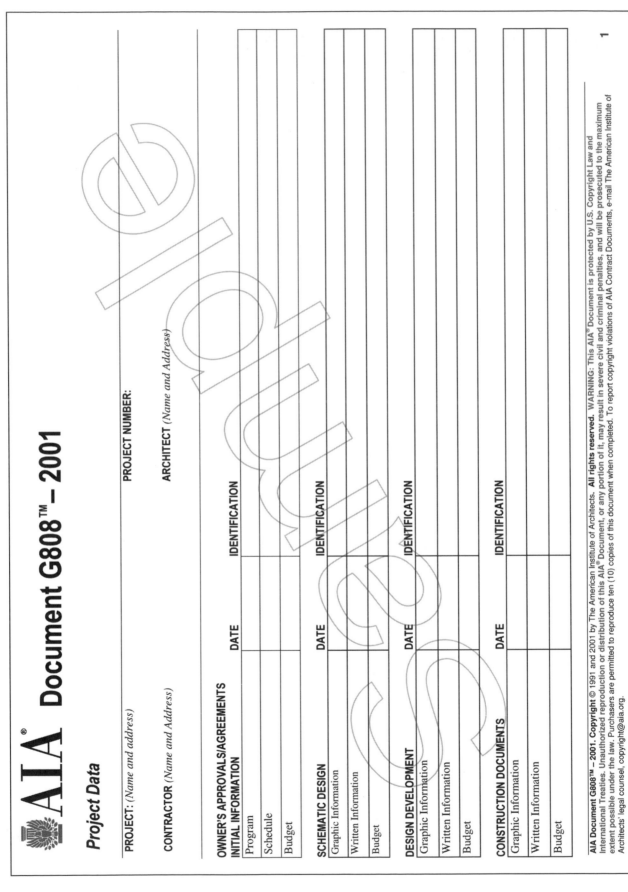

AIA® Document G808™ – 2001

Project Data

PROJECT: *(Name and address)*

PROJECT NUMBER:

CONTRACTOR *(Name and Address)*

ARCHITECT *(Name and Address)*

OWNER'S APPROVALS/AGREEMENTS

INITIAL INFORMATION	DATE	IDENTIFICATION
Program		
Schedule		
Budget		

SCHEMATIC DESIGN	DATE	IDENTIFICATION
Graphic Information		
Written Information		
Budget		

DESIGN DEVELOPMENT	DATE	IDENTIFICATION
Graphic Information		
Written Information		
Budget		

CONSTRUCTION DOCUMENTS	DATE	IDENTIFICATION
Graphic Information		
Written Information		
Budget		

1

ZONING ISSUES
Applicable Ordinances (*Number, title, and date*):

Property Identification (*Address, tax number, square and unit, etc.*):

Zoning District:

Proposed Use:

_____ Conforming _____ Non-conforming

BUILDING CODE ISSUES
Use of Adjacent Properties:

APPLICABLE CODES (*If different*): _____

TYPE	AUTHORITY WITH JURISDICTION	MODEL CODE (*Title and year*)	AMENDMENT TO MODEL CODE	REMARKS
Building				
Life Safety				
Accessibility				
Mechanical				
Plumbing				
Fire Prevention				
Electrical				
Elevator				
Other				

2

PROJECT: PROJECT NUMBER:

REGULATORY REVIEWS/APPROVALS

AGENCY/DEPT.	REVIEWER	DATE	PURPOSE	REMARKS

UTILITY SERVICES

SERVICE	CAPACITY	TYPE	PROVIDER	DATE CONFIRMED	REMARKS
Gas					
Water					
Storm					
Sanitary					
Fire Protection					
Power					
Telephone					
Data					
Cable					

3

PROJECT:

SEPARATION RATINGS *(If separated use is implemented)*:

Single Use of Single with Incidental (Accessory) Use   Non-Separated (Mixed) Use   Separated Use

PROGRAM FUNCTION	MAXIMUM CONTIGUOUS AREA	CONSTRUCTION CLASSIFICATION	SPRINKLERS PROVIDED

USE GROUP/OCCUPANCY CLASS *(See AIA Document G808A for help completing this section)*:

USE GROUP/OCCUPANCY CLASS	RATING *(Hours)*	REFERENCE

4

PROJECT: **PROJECT NUMBER:**

MASSING / PARKING / LOADING

MASSING	REFERENCE	FORMULA	ALLOWED AMOUNT	PROPOSED AMOUNT
Maximum Height				
Lot Coverage				
Floor Area Ratio				
Number of Units				
SETBACKS				
Front				
Side				
Rear				
Special (*Corner, etc.*)				
Allowed Encroachments				
PARKING				
Car Space Size				
Car Space Count				
Accessible Space Size				
Accessible Space Count				
Van Accessible Space Size				
Van Accessible Space Count				
Alternative Space Size				
Alternative Space Count				
Aisle Width				
Drop-Off Requirements				
LOADING				
Type and Size				
Count				
Type and Size				
Count				
Type and Size				
Count				

5

EGRESS PATH

CATEGORY	REFERENCE	FORMULA	MAXIMUM OR MINIMUM	QUANTITY	
				REQUIRED	PROPOSED
EXIT COUNT					
WIDTH					
Aisles and Corridors					
Doors					
Stairs					
DISTANCE					
Travel					
Common Path					
Dead End					
STAIRS					
Rise/Run					
Winders and Curved Stairs					
RAMPS					
Slope					
Distance Between Landings					
OTHER					
Emergency Lighting					
Areas of Refuge					
Escapes					

FIRE PREVENTION

	REQUIREMENT		
REFERENCE			
Alarm Requirements			
High Rise Code Requirements	Apply to this project	Require Annunciator System	Require Fire Command Station

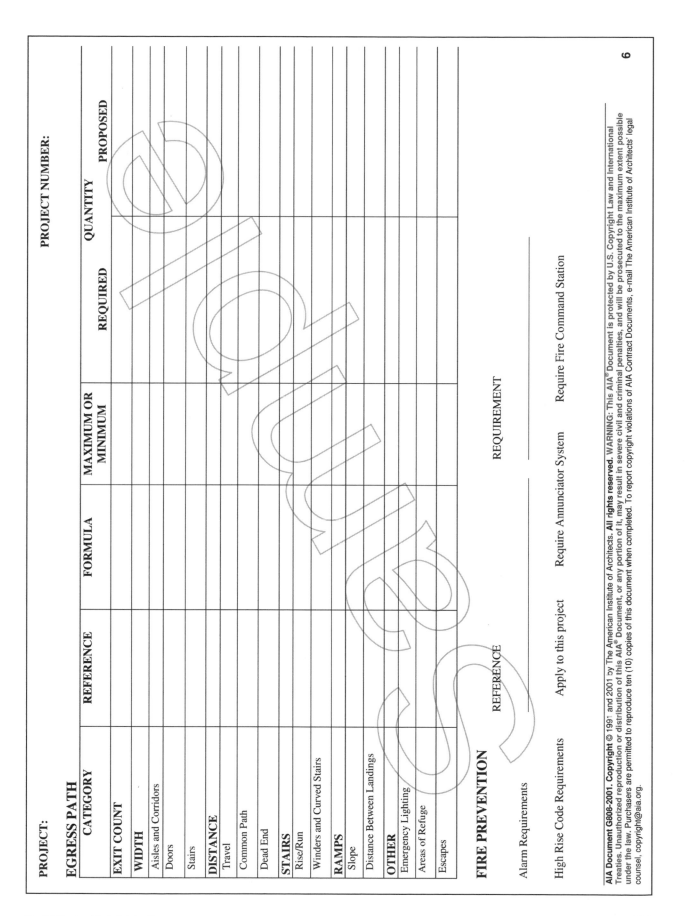

6

PROJECT:

PROJECT NUMBER:

MISCELLANEOUS PROVISIONS

CATEGORY	REFERENCE	FORMULA	MAXIMUM OR MINIMUM	PROPOSED	REQUIRED
HANDRAILS					
Height					
Diameter					
Distance Between Handrails					
GUARDRAILS					
Height					
Opening Size					
When Required					
LIGHT AND VENTILATION					
Natural Light					
Natural Ventilation					
Mechanical Ventilation					

PLUMBING FIXTURES

CATEGORY	FORMULA	OCCUPANT LOAD	TOTAL PEOPLE	REQUIRED		PROPOSED	
				TYPICAL	ACCESSIBILE	TYPICAL	ACCESSIBILE
Water Closets	Male						
	Female						
Urinals	1 /						
Lavatories	1 /						
Bathtub	1 /						
Drinking Fountains	1 /						
Service Sinks							
Showers	Male						
	Female						

7

Contract Administration G808A™ – 2001 Construction Classification Worksheet

PROJECT: *(Name and address)*

PROJECT NUMBER:

CONTRACTOR *(Name and Address)*

ARCHITECT *(Name and Address)*

PROPOSED HEIGHT

CONSTRUCTION CLASSES	SPRINKLER PREMIUM	HEIGHT/STORIES		HEIGHT ABOVE GRADE	
		ALLOWED	PROVIDED	ALLOWED	PROVIDED
Alternate 1					
Alternate 2					
Alternate 3					

PROPOSED AREA

CONSTRUCTION CLASSES	SPRINKLER PREMIUM	SINGLE STORY PREMIUM	UNLIMITED AREA	FRONTAGE PREMIUM	MULTISTORY PENALTY	AREA/FLOOR	
						ALLOWED	PROVIDED
Alternate 1							
Alternate 2							
Alternate 3							

8

PROJECT *(Name and address)* **PROJECT NUMBER:**

REQUIRED FIRE RESISTANT RATINGS

	ALTERNATE 1	ALTERNATE 2	ALTERNATE 3
Construction Classification			
Structural Frame *(Columns, Girders, Trusses)*			
Walls			
Exterior Non-Bearing			
Building Separation *(Fire and Party)*			
Separation of Uses *(Fire Area Separations)*			
Vertical Exit Enclosures *(Stairways)*			
Shafts			
Corridors			
Fire Partitions *(Tenant/Dwelling)*			
Smoke Barriers			
Floor Construction			
Roof Construction			
0'-15' *(Height above floor)*			
15'-20' *(Height above floor)*			
20' and above *(Height above floor)*			

FINAL DETERMINATION OF CONSTRUCTION CLASSIFICATION *(Transfer to AIA Document G808):*

9

Programming Report

Compile a project programming report by completing Parts A through D along with the programming questions, as required for project needs. Follow the instructions for each part, then organize in a project directory file; or maintain a hard-copy version of programming forms in a three-ring binder for review by project team and client/users.

Part A   Part A establishes the departments to be programmed. Complete this part with important contact and client information, as well as the basic list of departments.
 Note: Complete one Part A sheet only. A programming diagram may be compiled from this information.

Part A.1   Complete Part A.1, Department Diagram, by breaking down the client's company into departments for programming consideration. If the programming contract is for designated departments, use the diagram to denote areas within the department.

Part B   Complete a Part B sheet for each department or area. Complete a separate sheet for each department, describing overall department description and needs, and definition of required spatial adjacencies. List all rooms or spaces needed for that department.
Note: Part B sheets should *not* include common needs such as copy/mailroom or reception area.

Part C   Part C establishes and defines required public or common areas (all areas used by the public or by more than one department). Department heads, supervisors, and managers should review and fill out this form as a team to ensure that programming needs are met.
Note: Complete one Part C sheet only. Part D will accommodate individual space requirements.

Part D   Part D is the lengthy portion of the programming report; it contains the *most important* information. This documentation will be used by the architect, interior designer, and engineering consultants during the project design phases. Complete one Part D sheet for each space needed, from executive offices to storage closets. Color-code by department for ease of location.
Note: Produce a Part D sheet for each room or space. Sheets are formatted in both Word documents (Part D.1) and Excel spreadsheets (Part D.2).

PROGRAMMING FORM – PART A

To establish space requirements for the client referenced below, complete the requested information. The programming objective is to maximize the use of the square footage allowed without compromising the quality level of the client's needs.

CLIENT NAME:

Address	
Phone	Fax
E-mail	

Contact	
Title	Ext.

New Construction		Renovation		Both	
Approximate Square Footage Allowed					

Department List	

For Office Use Only			
Project Name		Project #	
Date		Initials:	

PROGRAMMING DIAGRAM

[Company]

Departments (Part A)

Common/Public Areas (Part C)

Lobby	Locker Room
Reception/Waiting Area(s)	Janitor's Closet
Public Restroom	Locker Room
Employee Restroom	Laboratory
Conference Room	Public File Room
Small Meeting Room	Library
Lounge/Breakroom	Print Room
Mechanical Room	Storage Room
Electrical Room	Copy/Fax/Mail Room

Sales Marketing (Part B)

Sales Mgr.
Asst. Mgr.
Open Offices
Graphics Room
Team Work Area

Purchasing (Part B)

Purchasing Manager
Asst. Mgr.
Open Offices
Storage

Payroll (Part B)

Payroll Mgr.
Asst. Mgr.
Open Offices
Lockable Storage

Business (Part B)

Reception
Operator
Check-Out
Open Workstations
Filing Area
Private Waiting

Administration (Part B)

Pres. Office
V.P. Office
Administrator
CEO Office
CFO Office
Asst. Mgr.
Executive Library

This is an example of how to break a company down into designated areas to determine the most efficient use of space and the relationships between departments and individuals. Departments are groups that have a common relationship with all the individuals involved and may have special areas or rooms that are used by personnel of that department only. For example, the company as a whole may have a public storage room, but Payroll will need a separate storage room that is lockable and accessible only to the Payroll Department. Also, in addition to the general reception area, the Business Office may have a separate, private reception area, which would be listed under the Administration or Business column.

PROGRAMMING FORM – PART C

COMMON AREAS

This form establishes and defines required public or common areas (all areas used by the public or by more than one department). Department heads, supervisors and managers should review and fill out this form as a team to ensure that programming needs are met.

Overall Mood or Aesthetic Desired

List of Common Rooms Required			
Lobby		Other:	
Waiting Area			
Public Restroom			
Employee Restroom			
Conference Room			
Smaller Meeting Room(s)			
Lounge/Break Room			
Library			
Storage Room			
File Room			
Print Room			
Elevator Equipment			
Electrical Room			
Mechanical Room			
Copy/Mail Room			
Computer Room			
Laboratory			
Locker Room			
Janitor's Closet			
Training Room			

For Office Use Only			
Project Name		Project Number	
Date		Initials	

SCHOOL FOR THE DISABLED

PROGRAMMING FORM - PART D2
DATE:

Room Name	Staff Specialist Office # 1	Room No.	STAFF-1
Existing Space	20 X 15	Adequate/Inadequate	Inadequate
Space Required	20 X 17 (24 X18)		
# of Users	1-10 (14-20)		

Description of Operations

As staffing specialists, we review files, schedule intakes and additional disability staffings, continuation staffings. Monitor compliance issues. Provide in-service training.

Activities Performed

Small staffings/meetings
Computer data Input
Report writing (memos, etc.)
Scheduling
Access/Read legal documents
File review
Conference calls
Intake start-up, procedures
Safeguards, consents
Evaluation review (Staffing teams)
Eligibility staffing/IEP development
Social history review
Training for small staff groups of 20
Play corner for children

Adjacencies Required

Visual	Physical
	Adjacent: CSC Secretary
	Adjacent: Staff Specialist Office #2
	Near: conference, copy, restrooms and storage.

General Finishes

Floor	Carpet
Base	Vinyl / Rubber
Walls	Soft/Light Colors
Ceiling	Acoustical

Workstation Requirements

Internet Access
Window

Furniture

Conference Table
Conference Chairs- rolling - 10 (20)
Desk
Desk Chair
File Cabinet
Bookcases
Computer Credenza
Trash Can
Credenza for Forms
Built-In Toy Storage
Play Area
Dry Erase Board

Architect's Note:
This form represents a combination of input from CSC Director & Staff Specialists. There seems to be two different concepts for this department. If we design larger offices for Specialists, then perhaps the large Central Conference Room could fulfill their remaining needs on a shared basis and we could increase efficiency.

Equipment

Computer
Printer
Telephone
Conference Phone
Lap Top Computer
Fax Machine
TDD
TV/VCR
Auditory Amplification Loop for deaf parents.

Technical Requirements

Lighting	Electrical	Systems	Plumbing	HVAC	Acoustical
Full Spectrum	6 wall outlets	Internet	N/A	Individual Control	Soundproof
Dimmable Lighting		Fax Line			
		TDD			
		Hands Free Conference			
Natural		Phone- 3 way			

Comments or Special Needs

Due to job responsibilities, we will need direct access to large conference room and have space available in office for small staffings. Staffings occur on a daily basis, 2-3 per day - simultaneously.

Architect's Note: No Cathedral ceilings.

SCHOOL FOR REHABILITATION

PROGRAMMING FORM - PART D
DATE:

Room Name	Room No.
HealthCare Supervisor Office	ADMIN-1

	Adequate/Inadequate	
Existing Space	None	I
Space Required	15 X 20	
# of Users	1-7	

Furniture	Equipment
	Computer
	Conference Telephone
	TDD

Description of Operations

Activities Performed

Adjacencies Required

Visual	Physical
	Adjacent: Administrative Secretary

Technical Requirements

Lighting	Electrical	Systems	Plumbing	HVAC	Acoustical
Full Spectrum	6 wall outlets	Internet	N/A	Standard	Soundproof
Dimmable Lighting		TDD			
Natural		Hands Free Conference Phone- 3 way			

Workstation Requirements

Internet Access	
Window	

General Finishes

Floor	Carpet
Base	Vinyl / Rubber
Walls	Soft/Light Colors
Ceiling	Acoustical

Comments or Special Needs

Architect's Note: Could use some help here. Could someone please provide desired information on this new position?

PROGRAMMING QUESTIONS – PART E

1. Is a reception/waiting area required? If so, how many guest chairs are to be accommodated? Are there special signage requirements? Will there be a build-in reception desk or just freestanding furniture? List other special requirements, such as a television, VCR, or feature wall.

2. How many offices will be needed? Any difference in size? Will they be furnished with new or used furniture? When possible, give measurements of each piece. Any special needs in any of the offices?

3. Will there be an open work area? If so, for how many cubicles and what size? New or used systems? Any specific departmental adjacencies?

4. Will there be a copy/mail area? What are the adjacency requirements? What type and how many pieces of equipment? Will built-in cabinets or counter space for paper storage, etc. be required?

5. Is there a need for a conference room or specialty rooms? If yes, for how many people? New or used furniture? Floor mounted outlets under table for communication/cable connections? (Note if this is an added cost.) Any need for a projection screen – manual or electric? Cable for television? Any other special requirements?

6. Will there be a break area or a larger lounge? Table and chairs? Is a door required to close off the area? Equipment needed, such as sink (single, double), refrigerator (with icemaker), dishwasher, garbage disposal, microwave, coffee maker, water cooler or insta-hot vending machine?

7. Any special or additional storage requirements? (Assume adequate storage will be provided for areas requiring basic storage.)

8. Will a separate file room be required, or will files be located in corridors or at individual employee stations? In general, how many file units and what size per user or space?

9. Will the electrical/phone closet be located in tenant space or in a central building location?

10. Will a separate computer room or closet be required? If so, about what size? Does it need to be adjacent to any specific area? What are the special requirements for this room?

11. List any rooms or special areas not previously noted. List any general comments about the space, such as location of windows, open or closed floor plan, etc.

Finish Specifications

Designers can use this specification sheet for their project-specific information or to provide specification details to others. Finish details are documented on the left; cut sheets or sample pieces can be placed in the box on the right. Change the header and use the same format for furniture specifications.

FINISH SPECIFICATIONS

CODE:

DESCRIPTION:

MANUFACTURER:

REFERENCE:

STYLE:

COLOR

FINISH:

SIZE:

LOCATION:

[*Insert sample in this space.*]

CODE:

DESCRIPTION:

MANUFACTURER:

REFERENCE:

STYLE:

COLOR

FINISH:

SIZE:

LOCATION:

ISSUE DATE: CLIENT: JOB:

REVISION:

Progress and Billing Reports Log

Project managers and project administrators, along with accounting department personnel, can use this log to manually document project billing and status of progress reports by phase, per month. One month is presented in this file, but worksheets are available for the year.

PROGRESS AND BILLING REPORTS LOG

Construction Documents

PM	Job No.	Project Name	Contract Issued Y	Contract Issued N	Contract Signed Y	Contract Signed N	Last Billing Date	Last Billing Amount	Progress Reports January 3	10	17	24	31
JQP	200109	Potomac	X		X		5-Jan	100%	X	X	X	X	X
JQP	200120	Perry	X		X		4-Nov	95%	X	X	X	X	X
JQP	200130	Sea Residence	X		X		5-Jan	85%	X	X	X	X	X
JQP	200149	Dock Office		X			4-Nov	$1,500	X	X	X	X	X
JQP	2002057	Haley Commercial	X		X		7-Dec	90%	X	X	X	X	X
JQP	2002105	Cottage - final payment	X		X		2-Sep	100%					X
JQP	2002135	Market Complex	X		X		4-Nov	100%	X	X	X	X	

Design Development

PM	Job No.	Project Name	Contract Issued Y	Contract Issued N	Contract Signed Y	Contract Signed N	Last Billing Date	Last Billing Amount	Progress Reports January 3	10	17	24	31
JQP	200102	Maine Bank		X					X				
JQP	2002093	Commerce Park		X			7-Dec	Hourly	X				
JQP	2003060	Office Park		X			5-Jan	Hourly	X				

Electronic Information Release

This release will serve as the transmittal that confirms the terms under which the designer releases electronic information to appropriate parties. It may be sent as an overall agreement per design contact or as an attachment for individual document transmissions. If documents are transmitted as hard copies, standard hard-copy transmittals found in other sections of the handbook may be used.

Date

Subject: Electronic Information Release for [Project Description and Project Number]

To: _____

The [attached/transmitted] Electronic Information for the project described above is proprietary and copyrighted. The misuse or unauthorized use of this information is strictly prohibited.

The use of this electronic information is restricted to the referenced project. The disk or material prepared from the Electronic Information shall not be used for other projects, or be transferred to any other party for use on this or other projects. Reuse or reproduction of the disc, data, or documents prepared from, by or with this disc for any other purpose or party for which the material was not strictly intended, is prohibited.

Recipient recognizes that information stored on electronic media, including, but not limited to, computer disk prepared by [Firm] may not be 100% compatible with their computer system due to differences in computer hardware and software, or may be subject to translation errors. In addition, recipient recognizes that designs, plans, and data stored on electronic media, including but not limited to the computer disk, may be subject to undetectable alteration and/or uncontrollable deterioration. If, for any reason, a conflict occurs between information contained in the electronic media and stamped, signed documents, the information on signed or stamped documents shall govern.

In consideration of the foregoing, the recipient recognizes and acknowledges that the use of such disk will be at their sole risk and without liability or legal exposure to [Firm]. No warranties of any nature, whether expressed or implied, shall attach to the electronic media or the information contained thereon. Furthermore, recipient hereby releases and shall, to the fullest extent permitted by law, defend, indemnify and hold harmless [Firm] from any and all claims, damages, losses and expenses, including attorney's fees, arising out of, or resulting from, the use of such disk, or data contained on such disk including, but not limited to, claims involving the completeness or accuracy of any data or information contained on the electronic media.

Notwithstanding [Firm]'s agreement to provide electronic information pursuant to this Agreement, nothing shall be construed to create contractual privity or benefit between recipient and [Firm], except as is necessary for [Firm] to enforce these express, limited terms and conditions.

Accepted by:

_____   _____
Authorized Signature   Date

CHAPTER FIVE

Bidding and Negotiation

Depending on the number of contractors involved, the bidding and negotiation phase can be cumbersome. But, now, with the use of laptops and spreadsheets, bid openings and calculations have evolved to a more streamlined process. Project managers and estimators can conduct bid meetings with the aid of preloaded, job-specific spreadsheets that not only save time, but also assure accuracy when calculating and estimating contract bids. These spreadsheets include:

Advertisement for Bids
Form for use with a general, open, or public bid. This announcement of project bid information can be placed as an advertisement or public notice in appropriate publications.

Notice to Bidders
Formatted for use with a private bid, this notice is for distribution to a preselected bidder's list.

Instructions to Bidders
Use AIA Document A701 as standard protocol to assist bidders as they prepare documentation for project bids.

Preliminary Pricing: Standard Procedure Outline
Guidelines for designers and contractors to use during preliminary project pricing process.

Pricing Worksheet
Spreadsheet formatted by product division and line item to calculate project pricing.

Register of Bid Documents
Use AIA Document G804 to track distribution of bid sets and addenda. (Note: When using this document, logging full name and delivery address is critical for follow-up with addenda and bid results.)

Preliminary Bid Comparison
Spreadsheet formatted to compare contractor bids. May be used to calculate both preliminary and final project pricing.

Addendum
Form for issuing project addenda.

Notice of Award Letter
Form to notify selected contractor of acceptance of bid.

Advertisement for Bids

Use this form for a general, open, or public bid. The template requires the insertion of project and bid information before it is placed as an advertisement or public notice in appropriate publications.

ADVERTISEMENT FOR BIDS

Sealed bids for the construction of

[PROJECT TITLE]
[PROJECT NO.]

at [LOCATION], [CITY], [STATE], will be received by [OWNER] at [LOCATION], [ADDRESS], until [HOUR] P.M. [TIME ZONE], on the _____ day of _____, 200__, and will then be publicly opened and read aloud.

The project consists of:

[PROJECT DESCRIPTION]

Bids will be received for a single contract including all work as specified.

Bidding documents may be examined at the following places:

1. [OWNER[[ADDRESS]
2. Construction Plan Room, [ADDRESS]
3. Construction Plan Room, [ADDRESS]

Bidding Documents may be obtained from
_____ Printing Department; Attn: Jane Doe
_____ [ADDRESS]
_____ [PHONE]
_____ [FAX]

Deposit of $_____ is required. If Bidding Documents are returned within five (5) working days after opening of bids and deemed to be in good condition, deposit will be refunded.

Return to:
_____ Printing Department; Attn: Jane Doe
_____ [ADDRESS]
_____ [PHONE]
_____ [FAX]

Notice to Bidders

Use this template for bids on private projects. Once the pertinent information has been added, the notice is distributed to those on a preselected bid list.

NOTICE TO BIDDERS

Date:

Project: Project No.:

Sealed bids for the construction of

at [location], [city], [state], will be received by [Owner] at [location],[address], until 2:00 p.m. [time zone], on the _____ day of _____, 200_, and will then be publicly opened and read aloud.

The project consists of: [description]

Bids will be received for a <u>single contract, including all work as specified</u>.

This project has a target percentage of [_] % for certified Targeted Small Business participation.

For more information contact: <u>[Name] [Address]   [Phone] [Fax] [E-Mail]</u>

Instruction to Bidders

AIA document A701 serves as the standard protocol to assist bidders as they prepare documentation for project bids, and this instruction sheet is the first part of the full bid documents package. Edit it to suit a public or private bid process.

Document A701™ – 1997

Instructions to Bidders

for the following PROJECT:
(Name and location or address):

THE OWNER:
(Name and address):

THE ARCHITECT:
(Name and address):

This document has important legal consequences. Consultation with an attorney is encouraged with respect to its completion or modification.

TABLE OF ARTICLES

1   DEFINITIONS

2   BIDDER'S REPRESENTATIONS

3   BIDDING DOCUMENTS

4   BIDDING PROCEDURES

5   CONSIDERATION OF BIDS

6   POST-BID INFORMATION

7   PERFORMANCE BOND AND PAYMENT BOND

8   FORM OF AGREEMENT BETWEEN OWNER AND CONTRACTOR

ARTICLE 1 DEFINITIONS

§ 1.1 Bidding Documents include the Bidding Requirements and the proposed Contract Documents. The Bidding Requirements consist of the Advertisement or Invitation to Bid, Instructions to Bidders, Supplementary Instructions to Bidders, the bid form, and other sample bidding and contract forms. The proposed Contract Documents consist of the form of Agreement between the Owner and Contractor, Conditions of the Contract (General, Supplementary and other Conditions), Drawings, Specifications and all Addenda issued prior to execution of the Contract.

§ 1.2 Definitions set forth in the General Conditions of the Contract for Construction, AIA Document A201, or in other Contract Documents are applicable to the Bidding Documents.

§ 1.3 Addenda are written or graphic instruments issued by the Architect prior to the execution of the Contract which modify or interpret the Bidding Documents by additions, deletions, clarifications or corrections.

§ 1.4 A Bid is a complete and properly executed proposal to do the Work for the sums stipulated therein, submitted in accordance with the Bidding Documents.

§ 1.5 The Base Bid is the sum stated in the Bid for which the Bidder offers to perform the Work described in the Bidding Documents as the base, to which Work may be added or from which Work may be deleted for sums stated in Alternate Bids.

§ 1.6 An Alternate Bid (or Alternate) is an amount stated in the Bid to be added to or deducted from the amount of the Base Bid if the corresponding change in the Work, as described in the Bidding Documents, is accepted.

§ 1.7 A Unit Price is an amount stated in the Bid as a price per unit of measurement for materials, equipment or services or a portion of the Work as described in the Bidding Documents.

§ 1.8 A Bidder is a person or entity who submits a Bid and who meets the requirements set forth in the Bidding Documents.

§ 1.9 A Sub-bidder is a person or entity who submits a bid to a Bidder for materials, equipment or labor for a portion of the Work.

ARTICLE 2 BIDDER'S REPRESENTATIONS

§ 2.1 The Bidder by making a Bid represents that:

§ 2.1.1 The Bidder has read and understands the Bidding Documents or Contract Documents, to the extent that such documentation relates to the Work for which the Bid is submitted, and for other portions of the Project, if any, being bid concurrently or presently under construction.

§ 2.1.2 The Bid is made in compliance with the Bidding Documents.

§ 2.1.3 The Bidder has visited the site, become familiar with local conditions under which the Work is to be performed and has correlated the Bidder's personal observations with the requirements of the proposed Contract Documents.

§ 2.1.4 The Bid is based upon the materials, equipment and systems required by the Bidding Documents without exception.

ARTICLE 3 BIDDING DOCUMENTS
§ 3.1 COPIES

§ 3.1.1 Bidders may obtain complete sets of the Bidding Documents from the issuing office designated in the Advertisement or Invitation to Bid in the number and for the deposit sum, if any, stated therein. The deposit will be refunded to Bidders who submit a bona fide Bid and return the Bidding Documents in good condition within ten days after receipt of Bids. The cost of replacement of missing or damaged documents will be deducted from the deposit. A Bidder receiving a Contract award may retain the Bidding Documents and the Bidder's deposit will be refunded.

2

§ **3.1.2** Bidding Documents will not be issued directly to Sub-bidders unless specifically offered in the Advertisement or Invitation to Bid, or in supplementary instructions to bidders.

§ **3.1.3** Bidders shall use complete sets of Bidding Documents in preparing Bids; neither the Owner nor Architect assumes responsibility for errors or misinterpretations resulting from the use of incomplete sets of Bidding Documents.

§ **3.1.4** The Owner and Architect may make copies of the Bidding Documents available on the above terms for the purpose of obtaining Bids on the Work. No license or grant of use is conferred by issuance of copies of the Bidding Documents.

§ 3.2 INTERPRETATION OR CORRECTION OF BIDDING DOCUMENTS
§ **3.2.1** The Bidder shall carefully study and compare the Bidding Documents with each other, and with other work being bid concurrently or presently under construction to the extent that it relates to the Work for which the Bid is submitted, shall examine the site and local conditions, and shall at once report to the Architect errors, inconsistencies or ambiguities discovered.

§ **3.2.2** Bidders and Sub-bidders requiring clarification or interpretation of the Bidding Documents shall make a written request which shall reach the Architect at least seven days prior to the date for receipt of Bids.

§ **3.2.3** Interpretations, corrections and changes of the Bidding Documents will be made by Addendum. Interpretations, corrections and changes of the Bidding Documents made in any other manner will not be binding, and Bidders shall not rely upon them.

§ 3.3 SUBSTITUTIONS
§ **3.3.1** The materials, products and equipment described in the Bidding Documents establish a standard of required function, dimension, appearance and quality to be met by any proposed substitution.

§ **3.3.2** No substitution will be considered prior to receipt of Bids unless written request for approval has been received by the Architect at least ten days prior to the date for receipt of Bids. Such requests shall include the name of the material or equipment for which it is to be substituted and a complete description of the proposed substitution including drawings, performance and test data, and other information necessary for an evaluation. A statement setting forth changes in other materials, equipment or other portions of the Work, including changes in the work of other contracts that incorporation of the proposed substitution would require, shall be included. The burden of proof of the merit of the proposed substitution is upon the proposer. The Architect's decision of approval or disapproval of a proposed substitution shall be final.

§ **3.3.3** If the Architect approves a proposed substitution prior to receipt of Bids, such approval will be set forth in an Addendum. Bidders shall not rely upon approvals made in any other manner.

§ **3.3.4** No substitutions will be considered after the Contract award unless specifically provided for in the Contract Documents.

§ 3.4 ADDENDA
§ **3.4.1** Addenda will be transmitted to all who are known by the issuing office to have received a complete set of Bidding Documents.

§ **3.4.2** Copies of Addenda will be made available for inspection wherever Bidding Documents are on file for that purpose.

§ **3.4.3** Addenda will be issued no later than four days prior to the date for receipt of Bids except an Addendum withdrawing the request for Bids or one which includes postponement of the date for receipt of Bids.

§ **3.4.4** Each Bidder shall ascertain prior to submitting a Bid that the Bidder has received all Addenda issued, and the Bidder shall acknowledge their receipt in the Bid.

3

ARTICLE 4   BIDDING PROCEDURES
§ 4.1 PREPARATION OF BIDS
§ **4.1.1** Bids shall be submitted on the forms included with the Bidding Documents.

§ **4.1.2** All blanks on the bid form shall be legibly executed in a non-erasable medium.

§ **4.1.3** Sums shall be expressed in both words and figures. In case of discrepancy, the amount written in words shall govern.

§ **4.1.4** Interlineations, alterations and erasures must be initialed by the signer of the Bid.

§ **4.1.5** All requested Alternates shall be bid. If no change in the Base Bid is required, enter "No Change."

§ **4.1.6** Where two or more Bids for designated portions of the Work have been requested, the Bidder may, without forfeiture of the bid security, state the Bidder's refusal to accept award of less than the combination of Bids stipulated by the Bidder. The Bidder shall make no additional stipulations on the bid form nor qualify the Bid in any other manner.

§ **4.1.7** Each copy of the Bid shall state the legal name of the Bidder and the nature of legal form of the Bidder. The Bidder shall provide evidence of legal authority to perform within the jurisdiction of the Work. Each copy shall be signed by the person or persons legally authorized to bind the Bidder to a contract. A Bid by a corporation shall further give the state of incorporation and have the corporate seal affixed. A Bid submitted by an agent shall have a current power of attorney attached certifying the agent's authority to bind the Bidder.

§ 4.2 BID SECURITY
§ **4.2.1** Each Bid shall be accompanied by a bid security in the form and amount required if so stipulated in the Instructions to Bidders. The Bidder pledges to enter into a Contract with the Owner on the terms stated in the Bid and will, if required, furnish bonds covering the faithful performance of the Contract and payment of all obligations arising thereunder. Should the Bidder refuse to enter into such Contract or fail to furnish such bonds if required, the amount of the bid security shall be forfeited to the Owner as liquidated damages, not as a penalty. The amount of the bid security shall not be forfeited to the Owner in the event the Owner fails to comply with Section 6.2.

§ **4.2.2** If a surety bond is required, it shall be written on AIA Document A310, Bid Bond, unless otherwise provided in the Bidding Documents, and the attorney-in-fact who executes the bond on behalf of the surety shall affix to the bond a certified and current copy of the power of attorney.

§ **4.2.3** The Owner will have the right to retain the bid security of Bidders to whom an award is being considered until either (a) the Contract has been executed and bonds, if required, have been furnished, or (b) the specified time has elapsed so that Bids may be withdrawn or (c) all Bids have been rejected.

§ 4.3 SUBMISSION OF BIDS
§ **4.3.1** All copies of the Bid, the bid security, if any, and any other documents required to be submitted with the Bid shall be enclosed in a sealed opaque envelope. The envelope shall be addressed to the party receiving the Bids and shall be identified with the Project name, the Bidder's name and address and, if applicable, the designated portion of the Work for which the Bid is submitted. If the Bid is sent by mail, the sealed envelope shall be enclosed in a separate mailing envelope with the notation "SEALED BID ENCLOSED" on the face thereof.

§ **4.3.2** Bids shall be deposited at the designated location prior to the time and date for receipt of Bids. Bids received after the time and date for receipt of Bids will be returned unopened.

§ **4.3.3** The Bidder shall assume full responsibility for timely delivery at the location designated for receipt of Bids.

§ **4.3.4** Oral, telephonic, telegraphic, facsimile or other electronically transmitted bids will not be considered.

§ 4.4 MODIFICATION OR WITHDRAWAL OF BID
§ **4.4.1** A Bid may not be modified, withdrawn or canceled by the Bidder during the stipulated time period following the time and date designated for the receipt of Bids, and each Bidder so agrees in submitting a Bid.

4

§ 4.4.2 Prior to the time and date designated for receipt of Bids, a Bid submitted may be modified or withdrawn by notice to the party receiving Bids at the place designated for receipt of Bids. Such notice shall be in writing over the signature of the Bidder. Written confirmation over the signature of the Bidder shall be received, and date- and time-stamped by the receiving party on or before the date and time set for receipt of Bids. A change shall be so worded as not to reveal the amount of the original Bid.

§ 4.4.3 Withdrawn Bids may be resubmitted up to the date and time designated for the receipt of Bids provided that they are then fully in conformance with these Instructions to Bidders.

§ 4.4.4 Bid security, if required, shall be in an amount sufficient for the Bid as resubmitted.

ARTICLE 5 CONSIDERATION OF BIDS
§ 5.1 OPENING OF BIDS
At the discretion of the Owner, if stipulated in the Advertisement or Invitation to Bid, the properly identified Bids received on time will be publicly opened and will be read aloud. An abstract of the Bids may be made available to Bidders.

§ 5.2 REJECTION OF BIDS
The Owner shall have the right to reject any or all Bids. A Bid not accompanied by a required bid security or by other data required by the Bidding Documents, or a Bid which is in any way incomplete or irregular is subject to rejection.

§ 5.3 ACCEPTANCE OF BID (AWARD)
§ 5.3.1 It is the intent of the Owner to award a Contract to the lowest qualified Bidder provided the Bid has been submitted in accordance with the requirements of the Bidding Documents and does not exceed the funds available. The Owner shall have the right to waive informalities and irregularities in a Bid received and to accept the Bid which, in the Owner's judgment, is in the Owner's own best interests.

§ 5.3.2 The Owner shall have the right to accept Alternates in any order or combination, unless otherwise specifically provided in the Bidding Documents, and to determine the low Bidder on the basis of the sum of the Base Bid and Alternates accepted.

ARTICLE 6 POST-BID INFORMATION
§ 6.1 CONTRACTOR'S QUALIFICATION STATEMENT
Bidders to whom award of a Contract is under consideration shall submit to the Architect, upon request, a properly executed AIA Document A305, Contractor's Qualification Statement, unless such a Statement has been previously required and submitted as a prerequisite to the issuance of Bidding Documents.

§ 6.2 OWNER'S FINANCIAL CAPABILITY
The Owner shall, at the request of the Bidder to whom award of a Contract is under consideration and no later than seven days prior to the expiration of the time for withdrawal of Bids, furnish to the Bidder reasonable evidence that financial arrangements have been made to fulfill the Owner's obligations under the Contract. Unless such reasonable evidence is furnished, the Bidder will not be required to execute the Agreement between the Owner and Contractor.

§ 6.3 SUBMITTALS
§ 6.3.1 The Bidder shall, as soon as practicable or as stipulated in the Bidding Documents, after notification of selection for the award of a Contract, furnish to the Owner through the Architect in writing:

    .1   a designation of the Work to be performed with the Bidder's own forces;

    .2   names of the manufacturers, products, and the suppliers of principal items or systems of materials and equipment proposed for the Work; and

    .3   names of persons or entities (including those who are to furnish materials or equipment fabricated to a special design) proposed for the principal portions of the Work.

§ 6.3.2 The Bidder will be required to establish to the satisfaction of the Architect and Owner the reliability and responsibility of the persons or entities proposed to furnish and perform the Work described in the Bidding Documents.

5

§ 6.3.3 Prior to the execution of the Contract, the Architect will notify the Bidder in writing if either the Owner or Architect, after due investigation, has reasonable objection to a person or entity proposed by the Bidder. If the Owner or Architect has reasonable objection to a proposed person or entity, the Bidder may, at the Bidder's option, (1) withdraw the Bid or (2) submit an acceptable substitute person or entity with an adjustment in the Base Bid or Alternate Bid to cover the difference in cost occasioned by such substitution. The Owner may accept the adjusted bid price or disqualify the Bidder. In the event of either withdrawal or disqualification, bid security will not be forfeited.

§ 6.3.4 Persons and entities proposed by the Bidder and to whom the Owner and Architect have made no reasonable objection must be used on the Work for which they were proposed and shall not be changed except with the written consent of the Owner and Architect.

ARTICLE 7 PERFORMANCE BOND AND PAYMENT BOND
§ 7.1 BOND REQUIREMENTS
§ 7.1.1 If stipulated in the Bidding Documents, the Bidder shall furnish bonds covering the faithful performance of the Contract and payment of all obligations arising thereunder. Bonds may be secured through the Bidder's usual sources.

§ 7.1.2 If the furnishing of such bonds is stipulated in the Bidding Documents, the cost shall be included in the Bid. If the furnishing of such bonds is required after receipt of bids and before execution of the Contract, the cost of such bonds shall be added to the Bid in determining the Contract Sum.

§ 7.1.3 If the Owner requires that bonds be secured from other than the Bidder's usual sources, changes in cost will be adjusted as provided in the Contract Documents.

§ 7.2 TIME OF DELIVERY AND FORM OF BONDS
§ 7.2.1 The Bidder shall deliver the required bonds to the Owner not later than three days following the date of execution of the Contract. If the Work is to be commenced prior thereto in response to a letter of intent, the Bidder shall, prior to commencement of the Work, submit evidence satisfactory to the Owner that such bonds will be furnished and delivered in accordance with this Section 7.2.1.

§ 7.2.2 Unless otherwise provided, the bonds shall be written on AIA Document A312, Performance Bond and Payment Bond. Both bonds shall be written in the amount of the Contract Sum.

§ 7.2.3 The bonds shall be dated on or after the date of the Contract.

§ 7.2.4 The Bidder shall require the attorney-in-fact who executes the required bonds on behalf of the surety to affix thereto a certified and current copy of the power of attorney.

ARTICLE 8 FORM OF AGREEMENT BETWEEN OWNER AND CONTRACTOR
Unless otherwise required in the Bidding Documents, the Agreement for the Work will be written on AIA Document A101, Standard Form of Agreement Between Owner and Contractor Where the Basis of Payment Is a Stipulated Sum.

Preliminary Pricing: Standard Procedure Outline

Edit this guideline to suit the procedures used by your design firm during the preliminary pricing process with the selected contractor. Consider making this form an element of the bid package by inserting it after the Instructions to Bidders form; or share it with the contractor upon award of the contract.

PRELIMINARY PRICING: STANDARD PROCEDURE OUTLINE

I. **PRELIMINARY BID DOCUMENTS**

    A. **Instruction to Bidders** (Edit instructions for this project)
    B. **Design Development Drawings** stamped "Preliminary/Not for Construction"
        1. Title Sheet
        2. Existing Topographical Map/Survey
        3. Site Plan
        4. Noted Floor Plan(s)
        5. Roof Plan
        6. Schematic Reflected Ceiling Plan
        7. Exterior Elevations
        8. Building Sections
        9. Basic Interior Elevations (major rooms)
        10. Schedules (door, window, room finish)
    C. **Preliminary Outline Specifications** (performance type)
        1. Edit as necessary.
        2. Review to note level of construction expected on project.
        3. Note allowance schedule.
        4. Substitutions: if submitting substitutions, contractor to clarify with addendum.
    D. **Preliminary Bid Worksheet and Disc** - All bidders are required to use.
    E. **Miscellaneous Documents**
        1. Soils Report
        2. Conceptual Grading Plan
        3. Other

II. **PROCEDURE**

    A. **Contractor Selection** (Single or multiple contractor scenario)
        1. Design firm recommends or refers contractors suitable for project; or,
        2. Owner introduces contractor to be included in the exercise.
    B. **Owner Sign-off on Design Development Package**
    C. **Distribution**
        1. Design firm meets with prospective contractor(s) to present preliminary bid documents (see Section I).
        2. Design firm explains preliminary pricing exercise purpose and procedure.
    D. **Contractor Examination and Review** (Question and answer period with designer and subcontractors, 2-4 weeks)
    E. **Contractor Submittal/Presentation to Design Firm** (Submitted per "Instructions to Bidders" procedure.)
    F. **Design Firm Review Period/Bid Qualification**
        1. Designer reviews contractor bids and contacts respective contractors regarding questions and bid clarification.
        2. Designer compares Preliminary Bid Comparison Sheets.
        3. Designer develops Preliminary Pricing Analysis report.
    G. **Presentation to Owner**
        1. Designer presents Preliminary Pricing Analysis and Preliminary Bid Comparison Worksheet to Owner.
        2. Designer recommends Contractor to Owner or suggests value engineering to align project with desired budget.
    H. **Follow-up with Contractors**
        1. Inform selected contractor.
        2. Inform remaining contractors of selection and recognize for time and efforts.

Pricing Worksheet

This spreadsheet is formatted by product division and line item for ease in calculating project pricing. Use it to calculate preliminary bid and final bid prices. Depending on the complexity of the project and bid, it can remain as one worksheet, or worksheets can be added to accommodate each product division.

PRICING WORKSHEET

	Project #:	Contractor:		
	Project Name:	**Estimated Project Duration:**		
		Cost	Option	Comments
	DIV. 1 - GEN. REQUIREMENTS			
1	Supervision			
2	General Conditions			
3	Temp Utilities			
4	Temp Toilets			
5	Temp. Telephone			
6	Temp. Facility			
7	Security Fence			
8	Scaffolding			
9	Equipment Rental & Maint.			
10	Special Equipment			
11	Construction Clean-up			
12	Final Cleaning			
13	Cartage			
14	Trash Hauling (Dumpster)			
15	Protection Materials			
16	Job Site Storage			
17	Contingency			
18	Pick-up List			
19	Special Inspections			
20	Material Storage			
	Subtotal: DIV. 1	0	0	
	DIV. 2 - SITEWORK			
21	Demolition			
22	Clearing			
23	Survey Layout / Staking			
24	Tree & Plant Salvage			
25	Rough Grading			
26	Site Drainage			
27	Finish Grading			
28	Utility Trench & Backfill			
29	Wall Backfill & Compaction			
30	Sewer / Septic			
31	Electrical Service			
32	Water Service / Meter			
33	Water Meter - Fire Sprinklers			
34	Fire Hydrant			
35	Cable & Phone			
36	Gas Service			
37	Pool / Spa			
38	Water Features			
39	Entry Gates/ Pilasters/ Operators			
40	Fences & Gates			
41	Wood Trellis			
42	Driveway			
43	Entry Court			
44	Tennis Court			
45	BBQ Grill			
	Subtotal: DIV. 2	0	0	
	DIV. 3. - CONCRETE			
46	Concrete Slabs			
47	Concrete Footings			
48	Concrete			
49	Exterior Flatwork			
50	Concrete Cutting			
51	Lightweight Concrete			
52	Termite Control			
53	Asphalt			
	Subtotal: DIV. 3	0	0	

		Cost	Option	Comments
	DIV. 4 - MASONRY			
54	Masonry Block Walls			
55	Retaining Walls			
56	Masonry Fire Box / Chimney			
57	Stone Veneer - Material			
58	Stone Veneer- Labor			
59	Stone Veneer - House			
60	Stone Columns			
61	Misc. Stone			
	Subtotal: DIV. 4	0	0	
	DIV. 5 - METALS			
62	Structural Steel			
63	Metal Roof			
64	Spiral Stairs			
65	Ornamental Iron			
66	Railings - Exterior			
67	Railings - Interior			
68	Metal Handrails			
69	Stairs / Railings			
70	Ornamental Sheet Metal			
	Subtotal: DIV. 5	0	0	
	DIV. 6 - WOOD & PLASTIC			
71	Rough Framing - Labor			
72	Rough Lumber			
73	Rough Hardware			
74	Finish Carpentry			
75	Finish Lumber / Materials			
76	Pick-up Carpentry			
77	Misc. Lumber Pick-up			
78	Cabinets			
79	Wood Beam Ceilings			
80	Architectural Woodwork			
81	Closets			
	Subtotal: DIV. 6	0	0	
	DIV. 7 - THERMAL & MOISTURE PROTECTION			
82	Below Grade Waterproofing			
83	Roofing (Flat Roof)			
84	Roofing Labor			
85	Deck Coating			
86	Insulation			
87	Sealants & Weatherstrip			
88	Sheet Metal / Flashing			
89	Gutters			
90	Skylights			
91	Shower Pans			
	Subtotal: DIV. 7	0	0	
	DIV. 8 - WINDOWS & DOORS			
92	Entry Door			
93	Garage Doors			
94	Wood Doors - Interior & Exterior			
95	Doors - Labor			
96	Sliding Doors			
97	Screen Doors			
98	Metal Doors - Material & Labor			
99	Wood Windows			
100	Windows - Labor			
101	Jamb Prep. - Material & Labor			
102	Metal Windows			
103	Wood Shutters			
104	Door Hardware - Finish			
105	Specialty Hardware			
106	Decorative Glass (Mirrors)			
	Subtotal: DIV. 8	0	0	

		Cost	Option	Comments
	DIV. 9 - FINISHES			
107	Stucco			
108	Drywall			
109	Painting			
110	Wood Flooring			
111	Ceramic Tile			
112	Stone Flooring			
113	Stone Tile @ Terraces - Material & Labor			
114	Bath Tile - Material & Labor			
115	Carpet			
116	Stairs & Handrails			
117	Wood Ceilings			
118	Countertops			
119	Interior Columns			
120	Fireplace Hearths / Surrounds			
121	Misc. Stone			
	Subtotal: DIV. 9	0	0	
	DIV. 10 - SPECIALTIES			
122	Bath Accessories			
123	Mirrors & Enclosures			
124	Fireplace			
125	Garage Storage Systems			
	Subtotal: DIV. 10	0	0	
	DIV. 11 - EQUIPMENT			
126	Appliances			
127	Labor			
128	Safe			
129	Kitchen Hood			
130	Laundry Chute			
131	Central Vacuum			
132	Misc. Equipment & Specialties			
	Subtotal: DIV. 11	0	0	
	DIV. 12 - FURNISHINGS			
133	Furniture			
134	Window Coverings			
135	Motorized Shade Equip.			
136	**Subtotal: DIV.12**	0	0	
	DIV. 13 - SPECIAL CONST.			
137	Radiant Heat			
	Subtotal: DIV.13	0	0	
	DIV. 14 - CONVEYING SYSTEMS			
138	Elevator			
	Subtotal: DIV.14	0	0	
	DIV. 15 - MECHANICAL			
139	HVAC Equipment			
140	Concrete Encased Ductwork			
141	Rough Plumbing			
142	Plumbing Fixtures			
143	Fire Sprinkler System			
144	Water Treatment			
	Subtotal: DIV.15	0	0	
	DIV. 16 - ELECTRICAL			
145	Rough Electrical			
146	Electrical Fixtures*			
147	Lighting Switch System			
148	Site Lighting			
149	Security System			
150	Intercom Prewire			
151	Stereo Prewire			
152	Satellite TV			
153	Telephone Prewire / Intercom			
154	Computer Network Prewire			
155	Structured Wiring Prewire			
	May remove (included in contr. budget)			
	Subtotal: DIV.16	0	0	
	PROJECT SUBTOTAL:	0	0	
	Contingency			
	Overhead & Profit			
	PROJECT TOTAL:	0	0	

Register of Bid Documents

Use AIA Document G804, Register of Bid Documents, to track distribution of bid sets and addenda. Use full names and delivery addresses when first logging in bidders to facilitate follow-up with addenda and bid results.

®AIA Document G804™ – 2001

Register of Bid Documents (Instructions on the reverse side)

PROJECT NUMBER: _____

PROJECT: _____

OWNER: _____

ARCHITECT: _____

RELEASE OF DOCUMENT DATE: _____

BIDS DUE ON (Date and time): _____

AT (Address): _____

ADVERTISEMENT OR INVITATION TO BIDDERS:

DATE PUBLISHED: _____

SOLICITATION TYPE: ☐ open ☐ invited ☐ list ☐ pre-qualified ☐ other

DEPOSIT: _____

REFUND: _____

FORFEITURE DATE: _____

SPECIAL INSTRUCTIONS: _____

ADDENDA (Indicate issue dates):

Bidder	1. Bid Received	Addenda Issued	2. Recipient (Company name, address, phone and fax numbers)	3.	4.	5. Deposit / Refund	6. Documents
						Date Received: $ Received: Date Returned: $ Returned:	Date Issued: # of Sets Issued: Dates Returned: # of Sets Returned:
						Date Received: $ Received: Date Returned: $ Returned:	Date Issued: # of Sets Issued: Dates Returned: # of Sets Returned:
						Date Received: $ Received: Date Returned: $ Returned:	Date Issued: # of Sets Issued: Dates Returned: # of Sets Returned:
						Date Received: $ Received: Date Returned: $ Returned:	Date Issued: # of Sets Issued: Dates Returned: # of Sets Returned:
						Date Received: $ Received: Date Returned: $ Returned:	Date Issued: # of Sets Issued: Dates Returned: # of Sets Returned:
						Date Received: $ Received: Date Returned: $ Returned:	Date Issued: # of Sets Issued: Dates Returned: # of Sets Returned:
						Date Received: $ Received: Date Returned: $ Returned:	Date Issued: # of Sets Issued: Date Returned: $ Returned:

1

Preliminary Bid Comparison Worksheet

This spreadsheet is labeled as the Preliminary Bid Comparison, but can easily be edited for the final bid record. As with the Pricing Worksheet, this spreadsheet is formatted by product division and the line item for ease in calculating. Depanding on the complexity of the project and bid, it can remain as one worksheet, or worksheets can be added to accommodate each product division.

PRELIMINARY BID COMPARISON

		Contractor:			Contactor:		
	Project #:	Estimated Project Duration:			Estimated Project Duration:		
	Project Name:	Low	High	Comments	Low	High	Comments
	DIV. 1 - GEN. REQUIREMENTS						
1	Supervision						
2	General Conditions						
3	Temp Utilities						
4	Temp Toilets						
5	Temp. Telephone						
6	Temp. Facility						
7	Security Fence						
8	Scaffolding						
9	Equipment Rental & Maint.						
10	Special Equipment						
11	Construction Clean-up						
12	Final Cleaning						
13	Cartage						
14	Trash Hauling (Dumpster)						
15	Protection Materials						
16	Job Site Storage						
17	Contingency						
18	Pick-up List						
19	Special Inspections						
20	Material Storage						
	Subtotal: DIV. 1				0	0	
	DIV. 2 - SITEWORK						
21	Demolition						
22	Clearing						
23	Survey Layout / Staking						
24	Tree & Plant Salvage						
25	Rough Grading						
26	Site Drainage						
27	Finish Grading						
28	Utility Trench & Backfill						
29	Wall Backfill & Compaction						
30	Sewer / Septic						
31	Electrical Service						
32	Water Service / Meter						
33	Water Meter - Fire Sprinklers						
34	Fire Hydrant						
35	Cable & Phone						
36	Gas Service						
37	Pool / Spa						
38	Water Features						
39	Entry Gates/ Pilasters/ Operators						
40	Fences & Gates						
41	Wood Trellis						
42	Driveway						
43	Entry Court						
44	Tennis Court						
45	BBQ Grill						
	Subtotal: DIV. 2				0	0	
	DIV. 3. - CONCRETE						
46	Concrete Slabs						
47	Concrete Footings						
48	Concrete						
49	Exterior Flatwork						
50	Concrete Cutting						
51	Lightweight Concrete						
52	Termite Control						
53	Asphalt						
	Subtotal: DIV. 3				0	0	
	DIV. 4 - MASONRY						
54	Masonry Block Walls						
55	Retaining Walls						
56	Masonry Fire Box / Chimney						
57	Stone Veneer - Material						

		Low	High	Comments		Low	High	Comments
58	Stone Veneer- Labor							
59	Stone Veneer - House							
60	Stone Columns							
61	Misc. Stone							
	Subtotal: DIV. 4					0	0	
	DIV. 5 - METALS							
62	Structural Steel							
63	Metal Roof							
64	Spiral Stairs							
65	Ornamental Iron							
66	Railings - Exterior							
67	Railings - Interior							
68	Metal Handrails							
69	Stairs / Railings							
70	Ornamental Sheet Metal							
	Subtotal: DIV. 5					0	0	
	DIV. 6 - WOOD & PLASTIC							
71	Rough Framing - Labor							
72	Rough Lumber							
73	Rough Hardware							
74	Finish Carpentry							
75	Finish Lumber / Materials							
76	Pick-up Carpentry							
77	Misc. Lumber Pick-up							
78	Cabinets							
79	Wood Beam Ceilings							
80	Architectural Woodwork							
81	Closets							
	Subtotal: DIV. 6					0	0	
	DIV. 7 - THERMAL & MOISTURE PROTECTION							
82	Below Grade Waterproofing							
83	Roofing (Flat Roof)							
84	Roofing Labor							
85	Deck Coating							
86	Insulation							
87	Sealants & Weatherstrip							
88	Sheet Metal / Flashing							
89	Gutters							
90	Skylights							
91	Shower Pans							
	Subtotal: DIV. 7					0	0	
	DIV. 8 - WINDOWS & DOORS							
92	Entry Door							
93	Garage Doors							
94	Wood Doors - Interior & Exterior							
95	Doors - Labor							
96	Sliding Doors							
97	Screen Doors							
98	Metal Doors - Material & Labor							
99	Wood Windows							
100	Windows - Labor							
101	Jamb Prep. - Material & Labor							
102	Metal Windows							
103	Wood Shutters							
104	Door Hardware - Finish							
105	Specialty Hardware							
106	Decorative Glass (Mirrors)							
	Subtotal: DIV. 8					0	0	
	DIV. 9 - FINISHES							
107	Stucco							
108	Drywall							
109	Painting							
110	Wood Flooring							
111	Ceramic Tile							
112	Stone Flooring							
113	Stone Tile @ Terraces - Material & Labor							
114	Bath Tile - Material & Labor							
115	Carpet							

		Low	High	Comments		Low	High	Comments
116	Stairs & Handrails							
117	Wood Ceilings							
118	Countertops							
119	Interior Columns							
120	Fireplace Hearths / Surrounds							
121	Misc. Stone							
	Subtotal: DIV. 9					0	0	
	DIV. 10 - SPECIALTIES							
122	Bath Accessories							
123	Mirrors & Enclosures							
124	Fireplace							
125	Garage Storage Systems							
	Subtotal: DIV. 10					0	0	
	DIV. 11 - EQUIPMENT							
126	Appliances							
127	Labor							
128	Safe							
129	Kitchen Hood							
130	Laundry Chute							
131	Central Vacuum							
132	Misc. Equipment & Specialties							
	Subtotal: DIV. 11					0	0	
	DIV. 12 - FURNISHINGS							
133	Furniture							
134	Window Coverings							
135	Motorized Shade Equip.							
136	**Subtotal: DIV.12**					0	0	
	DIV. 13 - SPECIAL CONST.							
137	Radiant Heat							
	Subtotal: DIV.13					0	0	
	DIV. 14 - CONVEYING SYSTEMS							
138	Elevator							
	Subtotal: DIV.14					0	0	
	DIV. 15 - MECHANICAL							
139	HVAC Equipment							
140	Concrete Encased Ductwork							
141	Rough Plumbing							
142	Plumbing Fixtures							
143	Fire Sprinkler System							
144	Water Treatment							
	Subtotal: DIV.15					0	0	
	DIV. 16 - ELECTRICAL							
145	Rough Electrical							
146	Electrical Fixtures*							
147	Lighting Switch System							
148	Site Lighting							
149	Security System							
150	Intercom Prewire							
151	Stereo Prewire							
152	Satellite TV							
153	Telephone Prewire / Intercom							
154	Computer Network Prewire							
155	Structured Wiring Prewire							
	May remove (included in contr. budget)							
	Subtotal: DIV.16					0	0	
	PROJECT SUBTOTAL:					0	0	
	Contingency							
	Overhead & Profit							
	PROJECT TOTAL:					0	0	

Addendum

As project bid documents are reviewed and clarifications are requested, use this addendum format to itemize and describe clarifications. It is important to number addenda consecutively and apply clarifications to the documents, as appropriate.

ADDENDUM No.

Project:

Project No.:

Bid No.:

Client/Owner:

Date of issue:

GENERAL   **The following clarifications are offered:**

Item 1.

SPECIFICATIONS:

Item 2.

DRAWINGS:

Item 3.

SUPPLEMENTAL DRAWINGS:

Item 4.

END OF ADDENDUM No. [   ]

Notice of Award Letter

Format this letter to notify the selected contractor of acceptance of bid.

NOTICE OF AWARD LETTER

[DATE]

Subject: Notice of Award for [project]

Dear _____:

The Owner has considered the bid you submitted on [date] for the referenced project. This letter will serve as notice that your bid in the amount of [dollars in words] dollars ($) has been accepted.

As required by the Bid Proposal, you must execute and deliver the contract agreement within [number] calendar days from the date of this notice. If you fail to comply with the requirement within the stated number of days, the Owner will be entitled to consider all your rights regarding the Owner's acceptance of your bid as abandoned.

You must return an acknowledged copy of this Notice of Award to the Owner and to [Designer].

Sincerely,

[Company Name]

[Signer's Name]

c: Owner

ACCEPTANCE OF NOTICE

Receipt of this Notice of Award is hereby acknowledged.

Firm: _____

Dated this _____ day of _____, 200__.

By: _____

Title: _____

CHAPTER SIX

Construction Administration and Post Construction

The successful management and satisfactory completion of a construction project depends on the successful organization and cooperation of the entire design and construction team. The documents included in this chapter focus on team communication and record keeping. A variety of formats are offered for the use of project managers, construction administrators and contractors to track day-to-day construction site activities; changes that may occur in the design documents and to the contract, including revision of tasks, products, costs, and schedule; as well as documentation to track project closeout.

Many firms now depend on electronic communication via project web sites to share the bulk of construction administration documents. If this is the case for your firm, share firm standards for electronic communication and record keeping with the entire construction team. In particular, share the guidelines with the team members who are authorized to fill out and post reports, note approval or rejection of change orders and submittals, or amend construction details in any way.

If construction documentation is managed via hard copies, a three-ring binder system containing copies of transmittals, meeting notes, review logs and various reports serves as an efficient reference support for the plans, product submittals, and samples that are filed in tubes and boxes, on or off the construction site.

One of the most efficient things a construction administrator can do is become a spreadsheet wizard. In many instances, the same information is required for more than one document. By coordinating a suite of documents, understanding the details of linking information, and discovering useful ways to sort and analyze the particulars, sought after information can be easily recorded and accessed.

None of the forms in this handbook should be used without the approval of firm leaders and reviewed by legal counsel experienced in design and construction. Firms with a national or multinational client base should be aware of and understand the varying construction-related laws from state to state, or country to country, and should review documents for project by project use.

Contract Amendment

AIA G606-2000, Amendment to the Professional Services Agreement, is to be used by the designer to confirm amendments to the contract for professional services. Changes to the contract fee and contract schedule are documented here.

AIA® Document G606™ – 2000

Amendment to the Professional Services Agreement *(Instructions on reverse side)*

TO:
(Owner's Representative)

Amendment Number:

In accordance with the Agreement dated:

between the Owner:

and the Architect:

for the Project:
(Name and address)

_____

Authorization is requested

    ☐ to proceed with Additional Services or a Change in Services.

    ☐ to incur Additional Reimbursable Expenses.

As Follows:

The following adjustments shall be made to compensation and time.
(Insert provisions in accordance with the Agreement, or as otherwise agreed by the parties.)
Compensation:

Time:

SUBMITTED BY:	**AGREED TO:**
(Signature)	*(Signature)*
(Printed name and title)	*(Printed name and title)*
(Date)	*(Date)*

Field Report

Use AIA Document G711-1972, Architect's Field Report, to document site conditions, project-based activities, and any actions required. Because field reports often are written on a daily basis and are, therefore, the most up-to-date record of project progress, this form is often distributed by e-mail or posted on a project Web site. Refer to the similar format of the Project Progress Report to decide which form best suits your project needs.

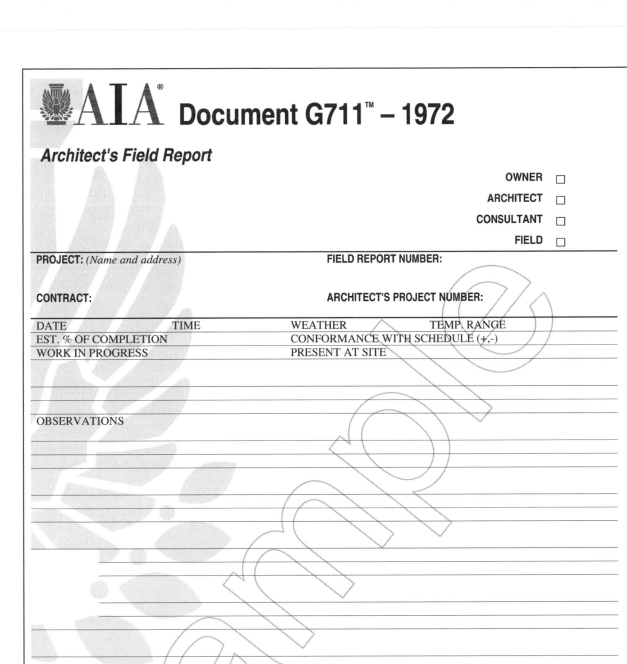

▲AIA® Document G711™ – 1972

Architect's Field Report

OWNER ☐
ARCHITECT ☐
CONSULTANT ☐
FIELD ☐

PROJECT: *(Name and address)*   FIELD REPORT NUMBER:

CONTRACT: ARCHITECT'S PROJECT NUMBER:

DATE   TIME   WEATHER   TEMP. RANGE
EST. % OF COMPLETION   CONFORMANCE WITH SCHEDULE (+,-)
WORK IN PROGRESS   PRESENT AT SITE

OBSERVATIONS

ITEMS TO VERIFY

INFORMATION OR ACTION REQUIRED

ATTACHMENTS

REPORT BY:

1

Project Progress Report

Project managers and construction managers can use this form to document project completion requirements, scheduled work results, and project-based requests and changes. Because project progress is often reported on a daily basis, this form may be distributed by e-mail or posted on a project Web site. Refer to the similar format in the Field Report to decide which form best suits your project requirements.

PROJECT PROGRESS REPORT NO. _____

Project:	Project Manager:
Project No.:	Start Date:
Client:	Contact:
Phase:	Report Date:

Consultant Deadlines

	Item	Targeted Date of Completion
Civil		
Mechanical		
Structural		
Plumbing		
Electrical		
Landscape		
Other		

Work Completed Since Last Report

Work Scheduled

Requests and Changes

Contractor's Monthly Report

This report is completed by the contractor and submitted to the project manager on a monthly or weekly basis, depending on the requirements of the project. The information in this report coordinates with several reports being produced by the designer's construction administration team.

CONTRACTOR'S MONTHLY PROGRESS REPORT

Project No.:
Project Name:
Contract For:
Report Period:

1 Work accomplished during the current report period.

Activity No.	Activity Description*	Period End Actual % complete	Comments

2 Work activities anticipated during the next report period.

Activity No.	Activity Description*	Period End Anticipated % Complete	Comments

* Attach copy of daily log with information required by section 01200 of Specifications

3 Pending RFI's

Contractor RFI No.	RFI Description	Date Submitted	Action needed by/Comments

4 Submittal Status

Date Submitted	Description	Date Returned	Status/Comments

Project No.:
Project Name:
Contract For:
Report Period:

5 Pending Change Order Proposals

Contractor Proposal No.	Description	Date Submitted	Action needed by/Comments

6 Delays Impacting Progress

Date Delay Started	Description	Date Delay Stopped	Cause of delay/Comments

7 Narrative

8 Construction photos included   Yes_____   No_____

9 Total estimated percent of contract work completed _____%

Additional Services Form Letter

Use AIA Document G605, Notification of Amendment to the Professional Services Agreement, to document additional services as requested by the owner. Insert related changes to project cost and project schedule. Prior to signature, review the legal ramifications of changes to project scope and services with counsel experienced in design and construction.

AIA Document G605™ – 2000

Notification of Amendment to the Professional Services Agreement
(Instructions on the reverse side)

TO: Notification Number:
(Owner's Representative)

In accordance with the Agreement dated:

between the Owner:

and the Architect:

for the Project:
(Name and address)

Notification is made of the need to proceed with Contingent Additional Services or to proceed with a Change in Services as follows:

The following adjustments shall be made to compensation and time.
(Insert provisions in accordance with the Agreement, or as otherwise agreed by the parties.)
Compensation:

Time:

Prompt written notice to the Architect from the Owner is required to discontinue the described service.

SUBMITTED BY:

_____
(Signature)

_____
(Printed name and title)

_____
(Date)

1

Additional Services Work Authorization Form

Use this authorization form or the Additional Services Form Letter to document additional services as requested by the owner. Insert all required information, being sure to identify changes to project cost and project schedule. As an alternative, consider using AIA documents G605 or G606, which deal with amendment to services agreements. Prior to signature, review the legal ramifications of changes to project scope and services with counsel experienced in design and construction.

ADDITIONAL SERVICES/WORK AUTHORIZATION FORM

No. [   ]

Owner/Client Name and Address: _____

_____

_____

Project Name/Description: _____

Project No.: _____

Date of Original Agreement: _____

Change Requested By: _____

Date of This Modification: _____

In accordance with the terms of the Agreement referenced above, *[firm name]* hereby provides confirmation of request for additional services by the *[Owner/Client]*. All of the Agreement terms and conditions shall remain in full force and effect, except as modified in this Work Authorization.

Description of Services: *[Enter description and note attachments, if any]*

Estimated Time Impact (in days or weeks):_____

Impact to Project Consultants: Structural____ Electrical____ Mechanical____
                                          Landscape____   Other_____

_____

_____

_____

Compensation for the additional services/work as described above is to be invoiced as:

Hourly, per contract terms____   Hourly, not-to-exceed $_____   Lump sum fee $_____

Submitted by: _____ _____
                        [Authorized firm representative]   Date

Approved by: _____ _____
                        [Owner/Client or authorized representative]   Date

Copies to:

Submittal Transmittal

Use this form to document the transmission of project product submittals, as well as the review and approval comments of the designer. Transmittals should be signed only by the duly designated, authorized person.

PROJECT NO.:
PROJECT NAME:

Submittal No.: _____
Supplier/Subcontractor: _____
Specification Section, Article, Paragraph: _____

Item(s) Submitted: _____

_____

_____

_____

Additional Information (Identify proposed variations and attach explanation in accordance with the General Conditions of the contract.): _____

_____

_____

_____

Approved .... ☐
Approved as Noted .... ☐
Revise and Resubmit .... ☐
Not Approved .... ☐
REVIEWED .... ☐

REVIEW is only for the limited purpose of checking for general conformance with the design concept of the project and general conformance with the information given in the contract documents.

APPROVAL of the data and drawings submitted will not relieve the contractor of responsibility for errors and omissions within the submittal, nor will approval relieve the contractor of responsibility for any deviation from the contract documents, unless the contractor has provided written notification that identifies and explains such deviations within the submittal.

Contractor is responsible for the following: quantities; confirming and correlating dimensions at the job site; means, methods, techniques, sequences and procedures of construction; and the coordination of work with all trades.

[Company name]:

Date: _____

By: _____
    [Authorized signature]

Submittal Log

On this spreadsheet, the project manager or construction administrator can trace the contractor's submission of specified construction projects. Note approval or rejection of the specified items appropriately.

SUBMITTAL LOG

Addition/Alteration to: [TITLE AND LOCATION]

CONTRACT NO.

SPECIFICATION SECTION

a	b	c	d	e	TYPE OF SUBMITTAL											CLASSIFICATION		CONTRACTOR SCHEDULE DATES			CONTRACTOR ACTION			CLIENT ACTION		
					f	g	h	i	j	k	l	m	n	o	p	q	r	s	t	u	v	w	x	y	z	aa
ACTIVITY NO	TRANS-MITTAL NO.	ITEM NO	SPECIFICATION PARAGRAPH NUMBER	DESCRIPTION OF ITEM SUBMITTED	DATA	DRAWINGS	INSTRUCTIONS	SCHEDULES	STATEMENTS	REPORTS	CERTIFICATES	SAMPLES	RECORDS	O & M MANUALS	INFORMATION ONLY	GOVERNMENT APPROVED	REVIEWED BY	SUBMIT	APPROVAL NEEDED BY	MATERL NEEDED BY	CODE	DATE	SUBMIT TO CLIENT	CODE	DATE	REMARKS

Shop Drawing and Sample Record

Use AIA document G712, Shop Drawing and Sample Record, to record shop drawings.

Shop Drawing Comments

As this form notes, shop drawings are to be reviewed by the designer and returned with applicable comments. This sheet provides for comprehensive review comments.

SHOP DRAWING COMMENTS

Date			Project No.	
Project				
To				

The attached shop drawings have been reviewed and are returned with the following comments:

ID No.	Spec Section No.	Rev.	Date Received	Submittal Title	Status*

*	Returned drawings are stamped with one or more of the following:	N	- No Exceptions Taken
		C	- Make Corrections Noted (resubmission not required)
		S	- Submit Items Specified
		R&R	- Revise and Resubmit
		R	- Rejected
		A	- See Attached Comments
		NC	- Not Checked

COMMENTS

Copies: _____

_____

_____   Signed _____

Request for Information

Use this form to document and define requests for information directed to the designer, as well as to record response or supplemental instructions. (Responses can also be documented on the following Request for Information Response form.) Requests for response may be initiated by the contractor or a consultant and forwarded to the designer. It is recommended that if contract fees or schedules change, either as an increase or a decrease, written authorization be requested of the owner and recorded.

REQUEST FOR INFORMATION

PROJECT NO.:
PROJECT NAME:

RFI No.: _____ _____ Date: _____ Requested By: _____

Requested of: _____

Drawing Reference: _____ Specification Reference: _____

Subject: _____

Information Requested: _____

_____

_____

_____

_____

_____

_____

Reply By: _____

Attachments: _____

Date Received _____ Date of Response_____ By _____

Response/Supplemental Instructions: _____

_____

_____

_____

_____

_____

_____

Distribution: _____

Note:
Response is to be followed without further notice unless the Supplemental Instructions recorded above represent changes in the contract cost or time. Contractor must notify the Designer within three (3) days of cost or time changes and must obtain prior written authorization before proceeding with Supplemental Instructions that affect cost or time.

Request for Information Response Form

Designers can use this form to document lengthy responses to requests for information (RFIs). As noted, it is recommended that if contract fees or schedules change, either as an increase or decrease, written authorization be requested and recorded.

RFI RESPONSE FORM

Date		Project No.	
Project			
To			
Company			
RFI No.			
Date Received			
Response Needed By			
Description			

COMMENTS

NOTE: Response is to be followed without further notice unless the instructions recorded above represent changes in the contract cost or time. Contractor must notify the Designer within three (3) days of cost or time changes and must obtain prior written authorization before proceeding with instructions that affect cost or time.

Copies: _____

_____

_____   Signed _____

Request for Information Log

This spreadsheet will become a valuable, chronological document that records the requests for information and the responses given. With RFI numbers duly recorded for reference to the original, detailed documentation, the information on this spreadsheet can be abbreviated to provide a snapshot report.

RFI RECORD - REQUEST FOR INFORMATION

PROJECT NAME   *enter name here*
PROJECT NO.   *enter number here*

RFI RECORD

RFI NO.	DATE REC'D	INITIATED BY	SPEC/ SECTION DRAW NO.	SUBJECT	CONSULTANT REVIEW				REPLY		
					SENT TO	DATE SENT	DATE RET'D		DESCRIPTION OF REPLY - OPTIONAL	DATE RET'D	REFER TO RFP/ CAR NO.
1	06/19/01	PUBLIC	PUBLIC	STRUCT STEEL CLARIFICATION	JONES	06/24/01	06/24/01		FIX IT	06/24/01	1
2											
3											
4											
5											
6											
7											
8											
9											
10											
11											
12											
13											
14											
15											
16											
17											
18											
19											
20											
21											
22											
23											
24											
25											
26											
27											
28											
29											
30											
31											
32											

Instructions to Contractor

Use AIA Document G710, Architect's Supplemental Instructions, to note minor instructions and clarifications that will not affect the contract fee or the schedule. If either will be affected, the contractor should notify the designer within a reasonable time.

AIA Document G710™ – 1992

Architect's Supplemental Instructions

OWNER	☐
ARCHITECT	☐
CONSULTANT	☐
CONTRACTOR	☐
FIELD	☐
OTHER	☐

PROJECT *(Name and address)*:

ARCHITECT'S SUPPLEMENTAL INSTRUCTION NO:

OWNER *(Name and address)*:

DATE OF ISSUANCE:

CONTRACT FOR:

FROM ARCHITECT *(Name and address)*:

CONTRACT DATE:

TO CONTRACTOR *(Name and address)*:

ARCHITECT'S PROJECT NUMBER:

The Work shall be carried out in accordance with the following supplemental instructions issued in accordance with the Contract Documents without change in Contract Sum or Contract Time. Proceeding with the Work in accordance with these instructions indicates your acknowledgment that there will be no change in the Contract Sum or Contract Time.

DESCRIPTION:

ATTACHMENTS:
(Here insert listing of documents that support description.)

ISSUED BY THE ARCHITECT:

_____   _____
(Signature)   *(Printed name and title)*

Instructions to Contractor Log

Use this spreadsheet to document and track designer's instructions to contractor. With ITC numbers duly recorded for reference to the original, detailed documentation, the information on this spreadsheet can be abbreviated to provide a snapshot report.

INSTRUCTIONS TO CONTRACTOR LOG

Date: _____
Project : _____
Project No.: _____

ITC NO.	Date of ITC	Instructions to Contractor	Date of Completion
1			
2			
3			
4			
5			
6			
7			
8			
9			
10			
11			
12			
13			
14			
15			
16			
17			
18			
19			
20			
21			
22			
23			
24			
25			
26			
27			
28			
29			
30			
31			
32			
33			
34			
35			
36			
37			
38			
39			
40			
41			
42			
43			
44			
45			
46			
47			

Supplemental Instructions to Contractor Log

Designers will use this spreadsheet to chronologically document the supplemental instructions given to the contractor. Record SITC numbers in column A as the reference to the original, detailed documentation.

SITC LOG - SUPPLEMENTAL INSTRUCTIONS TO CONTRACTOR LOG

PROJECT NAME   [enter name here]
PROJECT NO.   [enter number here]

SITC LOG

SITC NO.	DATE SENT	SENT TO	DESCRIPTION - SUBJECT	ATTACHMENTS OR SUPPLEMENTAL DETAILS	DATE RETURNED	REFER TO RFI NO.
1	06/19/04	PUBLIC	STRUCT STEEL CLARIFICATION	NONE	6/19/2004	
2						
3						
4						
5						
6						
7						
8						
9						
10						
11						
12						
13						
14						
15						
16						
17						
18						
19						
20						
21						
22						
23						
24						
25						
26						
27						
28						
29						
30						
31						
32						

Construction Status Report

This multipage spreadsheet is formatted to service a large project contract. File includes master construction change order status report, change order proposal log, change order logs for each discipline (general contract, plumbing contract, HVAC contract, electrical contract), a change order summary sheet, and an application for payment log. Summary sheets for other consultant contracts can be easily added to the file.

Construction Status Report - Change Orders

Project # :
Project Name:
Owners Representative:

Revision date:

Contract For:	General	Plumbing	HVAC	Electrical	Other	Total	Progress Estimates		As of Date:
Contractor:							Notice To Proceed Issued :		
Cost							Original Contract Duration :		
Original Contract Sum	$0.00	$0.00	$0.00	$0.00		$0.00	Original Completion Date:		###############
CO's Written to Date	$0.00	$0.00	$0.00	$0.00		$0.00	Time Extensions Authorized		0
Current Contract Sum	$0.00	$0.00	$0.00	$0.00		$0.00	Current Completion Date		###############
% Change From Orig.	#DIV/0!	#DIV/0!	#DIV/0!	#DIV/0!		#DIV/0!			
Pending CO Cost	$0.00	$0.00	$0.00	$0.00		$0.00	Number of Days Elasped :		$0.00
Projected Total Contract Cost	$0.00	$0.00	$0.00	$0.00		$0.00	Percent of time Elasped :		#DIV/0!
Gross SF									
Projected Cost/Gross SF							Schedule Update Data Date		
Payments							Update Projected Finish Date		
Total Earned To Date	$0.00	$0.00	$0.00	$0.00		$0	Estimated Days Ahead(+)/Behind(-)		$0
Total Paid To Date	$0.00	$0.00	$0.00	$0.00		$0			$0
% Paid To Date	#DIV/0!	#DIV/0!	#DIV/0!	#DIV/0!		#DIV/0!	Original Construction Contingency		#DIV/0!
Bal to Finish+Retainage	$0.00	$0.00	$0.00	$0.00		$0	Contingency Balance		$0

Contract Allowances

Allowance No.	Description	Quantity included in Bid	Unit Price	Total Sum included in Bid	Quantity Used	Referenced CO	Balance

Change Order Proposal Log

Project No.:
Project Name:
Contract For: General Construction Contractor: Date:

	Initial Documentation					Review								Comments
PBCL Log No.	Initiating Document Reference*	Contractor Proposal No.	Description**	Pending Amount Submitted	Time Requested (CD)	Date Received	To Consultant	Consultant Response	PBC+L To Owner	Date Owner Approved	Time Approved (CD)	Amount Owner Approved & Included in CO	Referenced CO No.	Status/Comments

Total Pending CO Cost	$0.00	Total CO Cost To Date	$0.00

* **Proposal Request No.** issued by _____, **RFI No.** issued by contractor, **Claim** issued by contractor.

** Include a complete and accurate description of scope of work, including revised drawings or bulletin drawings.

Change Order Proposal Log

Project No.:
Project Name:
Contract For: Plumbing Construction

Contractor:

Date:

Initial Documentation			Review									Comments
PBCL Log No.	Initiating Document Reference*	Contractor Proposal No.	Description**	Pending Amount Submitted	Time Requested (CD)	Date Received	To Consultant	Consultant Response	PBC+L To Owner	Date Owner Approved	Time Approved (CD)	Amount Owner Approved & Included in CO	Referenced CO No.	Status/Comments
				Total Pending CO Cost $0.00								**Total CO Cost To Date** $0.00		

* Proposal Request No. issued by _____, **RFI No.** issued by contractor, **Claim** issued by contractor.

** Include a complete and accurate description of scope of work, including revised drawings or bulletin drawings.

Change Order Proposal Log

Project:
Owner:
Contract For: HVAC Construction

Project No:
Contractor:

Date:

Initial Documentation					Review									Comments
PBCL Log No.	Initiating Document Reference*	Contractor Proposal No.	Description**	Pending Amount Submitted	Time Requested (CD)	Date Received	To Consultant	Consultant Response	PBC+L To Owner	Date Owner Approved	Time Approved (CD)	Amount Owner Approved & Included in CO	Referenced CO No.	Status/Comments

Total Pending CO Cost $0.00   **Total CO Cost To Date** $0.00 $0.00

* **Proposal Request No.** issued by _____, **RFI No.** issued by contractor, **Claim** issued by contractor.

** Include a complete and accurate description of scope of work, including revised drawings or bulletin drawings.

Change Order Proposal Log

Project:
Owner:
Contract For: Electrical Construction

Contractor:

Date:

Initial Documentation				Review									Comments
PBCL Log No.	Initiating Document Reference*	Contractor Proposal No.	Description**	Pending Amount Submitted	Time Requested (CD)	Date Received	To Consultant	Consultant Response	PBC+L To Owner	Date Owner Approved	Time Approved (CD)	Amount Owner Approved & Included in CO	Referenced CO No.	Status/Comments
		Total Pending CO Cost	$0.00								**Total CO Cost To Date**	$0.00		

* Proposal Request # issued by _____, RFI # issued by _____, Claim issued by contractor.

** Include a complete and accurate description of scope of work, including revised drawings or bulletin drawings.

Change Order Summary

Project No.:
Project Name:
Date:

	Initial Documentation					Review									CO & Contract Sum	
PBCL Log No.	Initiating Document Reference*	Contractor Proposal No.	Description**	Pending Amount Submitted		Time Requested (CD)	Date Received	To Consultant	Consultant Response	PBC+L To Owner	Date Owner Approved	Time Approved (CD)	Amount Owner Approved & Included in CO	Referenced CO No.	Change Order Total	Revised Contract Sum
General Change Order G No.																
Plumbing Change Order P No.																
HVAC Change Order HVAC No.																
Electrical Change Order E No.																
	Total Pending CO Cost			$0.00								Total CO Cost To Date	$0.00			

Application for Payment Log
Project:
Owner:
Location: **Project No .:**
                                                       Update Date:

Request No.	Date	Total Earned To Date	Retainage	Total Earned Less Retainage	Previous	Amount Due This Period	Balance To Finish Plus Retainage	Monthly Chg To Total Complete to Date
General Contract								
1								
2								
3								
4								
5								
6								
						Total Earned to Date		$0.00
						Total Paid To Date		$0.00
Plumbing Contract								
1								
2								
3								
4								
5								
6								
						Total Earned to Date		$0.00
						Total Paid To Date		$0.00
HVAC Contract								
1								
2								
3								
4								
5								
6								
						Total Earned to Date		$0.00
						Total Paid To Date		$0.00
Electrical Contract								
1								
2								
3								
4								
5								
6								
						Total Earned to Date		$0.00
						Total Paid To Date		$0.00

Change Order Proposal Log

This spreadsheet is formatted to record change order proposals, including cost changes, recommendations, and owner's action. This format will work well for small to medium contracts.

CHANGE ORDER PROPOSAL LOG

PROJECT NAME
PROJECT NO.

Change Order Proposal Log			COST									ACTION				
NO.	DATE REC'D	SUBJECT - DESCRIPTION	ADDITIONAL INFORMATION REQUESTED		NON-DISCRESIONARY CHANGES						DISCRESIONARY CHANGE	RECOM'D		DATE RET'D	OWNER'S ACTION	REF TO NO.
			DATE REQ'D	DATE RET'D	ARCHITECTURAL/ ENGINEERING COST	STRUCTURAL COST	MECHANICAL COST	ELECTRICAL COST	OTHER CONSULTANT COST	UNFORESEEN SITE CONDITION COST	OWNER ELECTED CHANGE, AMOUNT OWNER APPROVED	ACCEPT	REJECT		ACCEPT	REJECT
1																
2																
3																
22																
23																
24																
25																
26																
27																
28																
29																
30																
31																
32																
33																
34																
35																
36																
37																
38																
39																
40																
60																
CCD1																
CCD2																
CCD3																
BULN1																
BULN2																
BULN3																
BULN4																
BULN5																
BULN6																
BULN7																
BULN8																
BULN9																
BULN10																

Change Order History

The initial, comprehensive change order information is recorded on the Change Order Proposal Log. This spreadsheet documents the history of changes to contract amount per change order and calculates the percentage of change order sums to original contract sum.

CHANGE ORDER HISTORY							
	Date:						
	Project Name:						
	Project No.:						
	Contractor:						
	Project Manager:						
	Contract Amount:	$100,000					

CO No.	Amount	Date Approved	Change Code	Reason for Changes Summary			Percentage
1	1,000.00		3	1. Field Condition			0%
2				2. Design Change			0%
3				3. Client Request		$1,000.00	1%
4				4. Suggested by Contractor			0%
5				5. Design Omission			0%
6					Total	$1,000.00	1%
7							
8							
9							
10							
11							
12							
13							
14							
15							
16							
17							
18							
19							
20							
21							
22							
23							
24							
25							
26							
27							
28							
29							
30							
	1,000.00	Total CO's					
	1.00%	Percent of Contract					

Supplementary Drawings Record

These spreadsheets are formatted to document the history of supplemental drawings by discipline. Logs for architectural, structural, mechanical, and electrical disciplines are included in the file.

ARCHITECTURAL SD RECORD

DWG NO.	DATE ISSUED	DWG SIZE	TITLE OF DRAWING/REMARKS	REFER TO DTL/SHT NO.	ISSUED WITH ADDENDUM NO.
SA-1	06/19/03	8 1/2 x 11	COLUMN DTL	A100	1
SA-2					
SA-3					
SA-4					
SA-5					
SA-6					
SA-7					
SA-8					
SA-9					
SA-10					
SA-11					
SA-12					
SA-13					
SA-14					
SA-15					
SA-16					
SA-17					
SA-18					
SA-19					
SA-20					
SA-21					
SA-22					
SA-23					
SA-24					
SA-25					
SA-26					
SA-27					
SA-28					
SA-29					
SA-30					
SA-31					
SA-32					
SA-33					

SUPPLEMENTARY DRAWINGS - STRUCTURAL

PROJECT NAME   *enter name here*
PROJECT NO.   *enter number here*

STRUCTURAL SD RECORD

DWG NO.	DATE ISSUED	DWG SIZE	TITLE OF DRAWING / REMARKS	REFER TO DTL/SHT NO.	ISSUED WITH ADDENDUM NO.
SS-1	06/19/03	8 1/2 x 11	STRUCTURAL COLUMN DTL	S100	1
SS-2					
SS-3					
SS-4					
SS-5					
SS-6					
SS-7					
SS-8					
SS-9					
SS-10					
SS-11					
SS-12					
SS-13					
SS-14					
SS-15					
SS-16					
SS-17					
SS-18					
SS-19					
SS-20					
SS-21					
SS-22					
SS-23					
SS-24					
SS-25					
SS-26					
SS-27					
SS-28					
SS-29					
SS-30					
SS-31					
SS-32					
SS-33					

SUPPLEMENTARY DRAWINGS - MECHANICAL

PROJECT NAME   *enter name here*
PROJECT NO.   *enter number here*

MECHANICAL SD RECORD

DWG NO.	DATE ISSUED	DWG SIZE	TITLE OF DRAWING/REMARKS	REFER TO DTL/SHT NO.	ISSUED WITH ADDENDUM NO.
SM-1	06/19/03	8 1/2 x 11	AHU - 1 COIL	M100	1
SM-2					
SM-3					
SM-4					
SM-5					
SM-6					
SM-7					
SM-8					
SM-9					
SM-10					
SM-11					
SM-12					
SM-13					
SM-14					
SM-15					
SM-16					
SM-17					
SM-18					
SM-19					
SM-20					
SM-21					
SM-22					
SM-23					
SM-24					
SM-25					
SM-26					
SM-27					
SM-28					
SM-29					
SM-30					
SM-31					
SM-32					
SM-33					
SM-34					

SUPPLEMENTARY DRAWINGS - ELECTRICAL

PROJECT NAME *enter name here*
PROJECT NO. *enter number here*

ELECTRICAL SD RECORD

DWG NO.	DATE ISSUED	DWG SIZE	TITLE OF DRAWING / REMARKS	REFER TO DTL/SHT NO.	ISSUED WITH ADDENDUM NO.
SE-1	06/19/03	8 1/2 x 11	PANEL LIGHTING	E100	1
SE-2					
SE-3					
SE-4					
SE-5					
SE-6					
SE-7					
SE-8					
SE-9					
SE-10					
SE-11					
SE-12					
SE-13					
SE-14					
SE-15					
SE-16					
SE-17					
SE-18					
SE-19					
SE-20					
SE-21					
SE-22					
SE-23					
SE-24					
SE-25					
SE-26					
SE-27					
SE-28					
SE-29					
SE-30					
SE-31					
SE-32					
SE-33					
SE-34					

Contract Drawing Log

Use this spreadsheet to document changes made to the original project drawings during the construction administration period. Note that a Supplementary Drawings Record is provided to document any additional drawings that are produced during construction administration.

CONTRACT DRAWING LOG

PROJECT NO.:

PROJECT NAME:

Drawing No.	Description	Bid Set Date	Plan Revisions No.	Plan Revisions Date	Bulletin Drawing No.	Bulletin Drawing Date	Issued with	Revision Description

Conditional Waiver and Release upon Progress Payment

Use this form to document progress payments to the contractor. Note exceptions, if required, within the document as progress payments are made. And because lien waiver forms are specific to each state, have them reviewed by legal counsel experienced in design and construction and licensed to practice in the state where the project is located.

CONDITIONAL WAIVER AND RELEASE UPON PROGRESS PAYMENT NO. [   ]

Project:

Project No.:

Owner/Client:

Vendor/Contractor:

Upon receipt of a check from _____, in the sum of $_____ payable to [Contractor], and when the check has been properly endorsed and has been paid by the bank upon which it is drawn, this document shall become effective to release any mechanic's lien, stop notice, or bond right the undersigned has on the job of Owner located at _____ to the following extent.

This release covers a progress payment of the undersigned for labor, services, equipment, or material furnished to _____ through [Date] only and does not cover the following: any retainage before or after the release date; extras furnished before the release date for which payment has not been received; or extras items furnished after the release date.

Rights based upon work performed or items furnished under a written change order which has been fully executed by the parties prior to the release date are covered by this release, unless specifically reserved by the claimant in this release.

This release of any mechanic's lien, stop notice, or bond right shall not otherwise affect the contract rights, including rights between parties to the contract based upon a rescission, abandonment, or breach of the contract, or the right of the undersigned to recover compensation for furnished labor, services, equipment, or material covered by this release if that furnished labor, services, equipment, or material was not compensated by the progress payment.

Before any recipient of this document relies upon it, said party should verify evidence of payment to the undersigned.

Date: _____   [Contractor]

By: _____

Its: _____

Sworn and subscribed to before me this _____ day of _____, 20___.

_____
Notary Public

Conditional Waiver and Release upon Final Payment

Use this form to document final payment to the contractor. Lien waiver forms are specific to each state, therefore, have them reviewed by legal counsel experienced in design and construction and licensed to practice in the state where the project is located. Clarify conditions of disputed claims in this document.

CONDITIONAL WAIVER AND RELEASE UPON FINAL PAYMENT

Project:

Project No.:

Owner/Client:

Vendor/Contractor:

Upon receipt of a check from _____, in the sum of $_____ payable to [Contractor], and when the check has been properly endorsed and has been paid by the bank upon which it is drawn, this document shall become effective to release any mechanic's lien, stop notice, or bond right the undersigned has on the job of Owner located at _____.

This release covers the final payment of the undersigned for all labor, services, equipment, or material furnished on the job, except for disputed claims for additional work in the amount of $_____. Before any recipient of this document relies on it, the party should verify evidence of payment to the undersigned.

Date: _____   [Contractor]

                                   By: _____

                                   Its: _____

Sworn and subscribed to before me this _____ day of _____, 20__.

                    _____
                    Notary Public

Unconditional Waiver and Release upon Progress Payment

Use this form to document progress payments to the contractor. Note exceptions, if required, within the document as progress payments are made. Because lien waiver forms are specific to each state, have them reviewed by legal counsel experienced in design and construction and licensed to practice in the state where the project is located.

UNCONDITIONAL WAIVER AND RELEASE UPON PROGRESS PAYMENT NO. [   ]

Project No.:
Project Name, Description, and Location:

The undersigned has been paid and has received a progress payment in the sum of $_____ for labor, services, equipment, or material furnished to [Owner] for the referenced project and does hereby release any mechanic's lien, stop notice, or bond right that the undersigned has on the referenced project to the following extent.

This release covers a progress payment of the undersigned for labor, services, equipment, or materials furnished to [Owner] through [date] only, and does not cover the following: any retainage before or after the release date; extras furnished before the release date for which payment has not been received; or extras items furnished after the release date.

Rights based upon work performed or items furnished under a written change order which has been fully executed by the parties prior to the release date are covered by this release unless specifically reserved by the claimant in this release.

This release of any mechanic's lien, stop notice, or bond right shall not otherwise affect the contract rights, including rights between parties to the contract based upon a rescission, abandonment, or breach of the contract, or the right of the undersigned to recover compensation for furnished labor, services, equipment, or material covered by this release if that furnished labor, services, equipment, or material was not compensated by the progress payment.

Before any recipient of this document relies upon it, said party should verify evidence of payment to the undersigned.

Date: _____   [Contractor]

                                 By: _____

                                 Its: _____

Subscribed and sworn to before me this _____ day of _____, 20__.

                                 _____
                                 Notary Public

Unconditional Waiver and Release upon Final Payment

Use this form to document final payment to the contractor. Lien waiver forms are specific to each state, therefore, have them reviewed by legal counsel experienced in design and construction and licensed to practice in the state where the project is located. If applicable, clarify conditions of disputed claims in this document.

UNCONDITIONAL WAIVER AND RELEASE UPON FINAL PAYMENT

Project No.:
Project Name, Description, and Location:

The undersigned has been paid-in-full for all labor, services, equipment, or material furnished to Owner on the project, and does hereby waive and release any right to a mechanic's lien, stop notice, or any right against a labor and material bond on the project, except for disputed claims for extra work in the amount of $ _____

This release covers the final payment of the undersigned.

Date: _____   [Contractor]

                                  By: _____

                                  Its: _____

Subscribed and sworn to before me this _____ day of _____, 20__.

                         _____
                         Notary Public

Punch List

The format for this form is similar to that of the Meeting Notes. It serves as the record of the designer's review of construction. Prepare the document in anticipation of project closeout and distribute it to the design team and the general contractor. The designer should note items requiring correction, change, or completion in a consistent and straightforward manner. It is recommended that each punch list be numbered and that items be assigned consecutive numbers for ease of reference. Usually, the project manager is responsible for follow-up with the general contractor.

PUNCH LIST
NO. [   ]

Project:		**Project No.:**
Date:	**Notes By:**	**File No.:**
Architect/Engineer:	**Contractor:**	**Other:**

The following items were observed on site and must be completed or corrected by [date]. The General Contractor is required to coordinate all work with contracted consultants.

Master Bath - Room 1:
  1. Address scratch on left top edge of tub surround.
  2. Install tub diverter (Tuesday, May 27, 2004, scheduled by J.L.)

Master Bedroom - Room 2:
  3. Address interior finish on window sashes.
  4. Repaint on mechanical return mushroom (color number [   ]).

Den - Room 3:
  5. Adjust kick base of cabinets on the right and left sides of fireplace.
  6. Repair crack in sheet rock in upper west wall.

Kitchen – Room 4:
  7. Repair water damage in skylight well.
  8. Repair delaminating on the south side of the island.

Garage Bathroom – Room 5:
  9. Repair cracked floor tile.

Exterior:
  10. Install two (2) exterior hose bibs in the back pool patio area – verify location with owner.
  11. Remove spots of deck stain on north wall of upper deck.

General Notes:

  12. Clean all tracks for sliders and associated screens thoroughly.
  13. Adjust all interior double doors and catches.
  14. Remove paint from hinges and latches throughout.

Attachments:
Distribution:

Closeout Documentation Check List

Edit this check list to include and verify status of certificates, drawings, contacts, and manuals at project closeout. Responsibility for compiling such a list is generally that of the project or construction manager.

CLOSEOUT DOCUMENTATION CHECK LIST

Project: _____   Project #: _____

Contractor: _____   Substantial Completion Date: _____

Copies of the following documents should be completed to accompany the final Application for Payment as noted below by asterisks. When completed, the original checklist and original documents are to be filed with the project records.

_____   1.*   Fully executed Certificate of Substantial Completion, with attached punch list.

_____   2.*   Fully executed Final Change Order.

_____   3.   Final approved Application for Payment.

_____   4.**   Consent of Surety to Final Payment.

_____   5.**   Contractor's Affidavit of Release of Liens, properly signed and notarized.

_____   6.**   Contractor's Affidavit of Payment of Debits and Claims, signed and notarized.

_____   7.**   Properly executed Release of Liens by subcontractors and vendors.

_____   8.**   Certificate of Occupancy from proper municipality.

_____   9.**   Contractor's One-Year Warranty, properly notarized.

_____   10.   Warranty summary sheet and original warranties for items specific to this project.

_____   11.*   Contractor's certification letter per General Conditions of the Contract.

_____   12.**   Contractor's certification stating that no asbestos-containing materials were used on the project.

_____   13.**   Architect/Engineer certification letter regarding asbestos, per EPA regulations,

_____   14.**   Architect's and MEP Engineer's certification letter stating punch list is complete, work is per contract requirements, and recommending final payment be made to Contractor.

_____   15.**   Architect/Engineer's letter regarding liquidated damages.

_____   16.   Transmittal indicating keys have been given to project Owner, signed by Project Manager or Principal.

_____   17.   Final list of all subcontractors with contacts, addresses, and phone numbers, including emergency numbers.

_____   18.   Record drawings received from A/E and cover letter from Architect of Record and appropriate Engineer(s) stating they have reviewed the drawings and that they are as complete and as accurate as possible.

_____   19.*   Operations and maintenance manuals with cover letter from Architect/Engineer stating they have been reviewed and are complete.

_____ 20.*   Certified Testing and Balancing Report for HVAC System with cover letter from consulting engineer indicating the system has been reviewed and is approved.

_____ 21.   List of air handling units and related room numbers with schedule for and record of replacement parts.

_____ 22.   Finish Hardware Bidding List from hardware supplier through General Contractor.

_____ 23.   Copy of Punch List checked by contractor and approved by designer.

_____ 24.   List of all maintenance stock with attached executed transmittal from Contractor.

Signature [Principal] [Project Manager]   **Date**

*   Copy of cover document only to be attached to final application for payment and filed with project accounting records.
** Copy of entire document to be attached to final application for payment and filed with project accounting records.

Project Closeout Form

This simple form is designed to support project managers, administrators, and marketing personnel in the completion of project closeout items. An alternative document for project closeout is the AIA document G809, Project Abstract.

PROJECT CLOSEOUT FORM

Project No.

Client: _____   Phone: _____
Address: _____   Fax: _____
_____   E-mail: _____
_____

Project Location: Design Team:

_____   _____
_____   _____
_____   _____
_____   _____

Contractor: _____   Phone: _____
Address: _____   Fax: _____
_____   E-mail: _____
_____

Description of project: Total construction cost: $_____
                                                        Total design fees: $ _____
_____   Total consultant fees: $ _____
_____   Start up date: _____
_____   Close out date:_____
_____

                    Names   Services
Consultants:

_____   _____
_____   _____
_____   _____
_____   _____
_____   _____

Subcontractors:

_____   _____
_____   _____
_____   _____
_____   _____
_____   _____

Photography: Scheduled_____   Complete____

Press Release: Scheduled_____   Complete____

Inserted on web site: Scheduled_____   Complete____

Permission from client for publication: Permission on file_____ Dated_____

Request for Plans or Project Information

Use this form to document the request for and transmittal of project plans or other project related information. Such requests often come from owners, consultants and users. In all cases, no information should be released without the prior knowledge of the owner. If plans are transmitted electronically, refer to the Electronic Information Release found in Chapter Four of this handbook.

REQUEST FOR PLANS/PROJECT INFORMATION

Date: _____ / _____ / _____

1. **PROJECT IDENTIFICATION**
   Job Number: _____ (Job Number is required to locate files)
   Name: _____
   Address: _____
   City: _____ State: _____ Zip: _____
   Date Built: _____ / _____ / _____

2. **INDIVIDUAL REQUESTING INFORMATION**
   Name: _____
   Address: _____
   City: _____ State: _____ Zip: _____
   Phone No.: (_____) _____ - _____
   Fax No.: (_____) _____ - _____

3. **SEND TO**
   Name: _____
   Address: _____
   City: _____ State: _____ Zip: _____
   Phone No.: (_____) _____ - _____

4. **PURPOSE OF REQUEST**
   _____
   _____
   _____

5. **INFORMATION REQUESTED** (Specify exact information and number of copies needed.)
   _____
   _____
   _____

6. Minimum fee for the cost of researching files and documents is $[   ].
   Additional charges related to reproduction or storage retrieval may apply and are due upon receipt of documents.

   RETRIEVAL FEE   **$0.00**
   Make checks payable to: [Designer]

   ADDITIONAL CHARGES

Quantity	Item	Rate		
	Blueprints or Copies	$	/sheet	$
	Labor	$	/hour	$
	Delivery Charges	$		$

Total Due	**$0.00**

   Note: [Designer] reserves the right to provide copies at our discretion. Drawings are considered instruments of service and [Designer] shall be deemed author and retains all legal rights, including copyright.

APPENDIX

Resources

The following publications are recommended as "must haves" for your reference library.

Manhard, Stephen J. *The Goof-Proofer: How to Avoid the 41 Most Embarrassing Errors in Your Speaking and Writing* (New York: Collier Books), 1987.

Roget's Thesaurus (New York: Smithmark Publishers), 1999.

Sabin, William A. *The Gregg Reference Manual*, 9th ed. (New York: McGraw-Hill), 1999.

Strunk, William Jr. *The Elements of Style*, 4th ed. (Boston: Allyn and Bacon), 1999.

The following professional organizations provide management tools and educational opportunities to their membership and the general public. Most have a series of contracts, project forms, and administrative documentation available through subscription services or software purchase.

American Council of Engineering Companies (ACEC): www.acec.org

American Institute of Architects (AIA): www.aia.org

American Institute of Constructors (AIC): www.aicnet.org

American Society of Civil Engineers (ASCE): www.asce.org

American Society of Interior Designers (ASID): www.asid.org

American Society of Landscape Architects (ASLA): www.asla.org

Construction Specifications Institute (CSI) www.csinet.org

International Interior Design Association (IIDA): www.iida.org

National Society of Professional Engineers (NSPE): www.nspe.org

Society for Marketing Professional Services (SMPS): www.smps.org

Financial software for professional services firms often integrates project management programs with accounting systems to support day-to-day project management and long-term planning. Some of the most-used packages within the design industry are listed here.

Axium Software: www.axiumae.com

BST Consultants: www.bstconsultants.com

Deltek: www.deltek.com

Peachtree: www.peachtree.com

Primavera Systems, Inc.: www.primavera.com

QuickBooks Accounting: www.quickbooks.com

Semaphore: www.sema4.com

S3PS, Inc.: www.s3psinc.com

Timberline: www.timberline.com

Wind2 Software, Inc.: www.wind2.com

Professional services' management consultants are excellent resources for project-related documentation. Research through the Architectural Engineering Management Association (www.aema.biz) for a certified consultant near you, or refer to the nationally recognized firms listed here.

FMI Corporation: www.fminet.com

PSMJ Resources, Inc.: www.psmj.com

ZweigWhite: www.zweigwhite.com

Index

WILEY